Pagan Portals
Helenic Paganism

Pagan Portals
Helenic Paganism

Samantha Leaver

MOON
BOOKS

Winchester, UK
Washington, USA

JOHN HUNT PUBLISHING

First published by Moon Books, 2021
Moon Books is an imprint of John Hunt Publishing Ltd., No. 3 East Street, Alresford
Hampshire SO24 9EE, UK
office@jhpbooks.net
www.johnhuntpublishing.com
www.moon-books.net

For distributor details and how to order please visit the 'Ordering' section on our website.

Text copyright: Samantha Leaver 2019

ISBN: 978 1 78904 323 5
978 1 78904 324 2 (ebook)
Library of Congress Control Number: 2019955388

A CIP catalogue record for this book is available from the British Library.

Design: Stuart Davies

UK: Printed and bound by CPI Group (UK) Ltd, Croydon, CR0 4YY
US: Printed and bound by Thomson-Shore, 7300 West Joy Road, Dexter, MI 48130

We operate a distinctive and ethical publishing philosophy in
all areas of our business, from our global network of authors to
production and worldwide distribution.

Contents

About the Author

My name is Samantha Leaver, known to my friends as Sam, I live in the UK with my husband and Fischers Lovebird, Astro. I am as Anglo-Saxon as they come with blonde hair and blue eyes, however, I honestly believe a part of my soul was born in the Mediterranean.

Imagine a child, around about six years old sitting with her grandfather listening to tales of Heroes, Creatures, Gods and Goddesses. There, in the coastal town of Southampton on the south coast of England, I began my love affair with the Greeks. Fast forward a few years and I had very much rejected the path of mainstream religion. I found Paganism and eventually Kitchen Witchcraft, and I was still devouring anything I could find on Ancient Greece. It's worth noting now that I am not a historian or an academic; I have a long-held fascination with Ancient Greece and a deepening connection to the Gods of the Greek pantheon.

Following breadcrumbs, connecting dots, reading, trial and error, instinct, devotion and belief is where I thrive. I have a strong sense that I've just described a lot of other witches and pagans. I've settled in nicely with the Greeks, but I suspect this mindset could be applied to many other Polytheistic paths be they Germanic, Egyptian, Roman, Icelandic, or Slavic to name but a few.

Part 1 – Introduction

What is in this book?

Hellenic Paganism has seen both a growth in interest and an increase in people identifying with the tradition for several years. It is steadily becoming a strong presence under the umbrella of Paganism. As with most paths there are many differing practices in the Hellenic world, all underpinned by the values and ethics of what we understand to be the Hellenic way of life. This includes practitioners who simply believe and work with the Theoi (Gods) to those that attempt the daunting task of reconstructing this beautifully rich and consuming religion to the best of their ability, whilst, at the same time, being mindful of our modern way of life.

This book aims to explore the revitalisation and modernisation of ancient Greek life and looks at topics such as; myths and legends of deity, creatures and heroes, explorations of how the world works, calendars of individual Polis, Attic festivities and practices within and without the home, and, finally, the influence of magic and mysticism, mystery cults, and, Oracles.

This book hopes to show how research, dedication, observation of the world around us and, most importantly, intuition and practice can be applied to any path. The religious life of the Greeks was not considered separate to their everyday existence, the Theoi and their influence continue to survive in our modern world both in Greece and across the globe. The reach of this influence is not only astonishing, it is pure magic.

The Hellenes

The Graeci as the Romans called them, or Hellenes as they called themselves, were a group native to Greece or Hellas. The Hellenes were also native to Cyprus, Italy, Turkey, Egypt and Southern Albanian and, to a lesser degree, other countries surrounding the Mediterranean Sea. There were even Greeks as far west as France in ancient times. Today there are people who identify ethnically as Hellene all over the globe, Greek communities have sprung up on every continent on the planet.

Greece has had an influence on many of our cultures. They traded with many different people. They took to the seas with their ideas to find new lands. They started a way of life that has stood the test of time and can still be seen in our lives today. About 2,500 years ago Greece was a magnet for peoples of the ancient world, attracting and cultivating great thinkers, writers, artists, philosophers and politicians: you've probably come across at least one if you've read a little bit of history. They also had actors, architects, athletes and Greek society witnessed the emergence of medicine and the medical profession.

There have been people existing in Hellas for over 40,000 years, the earliest people being hunter-gatherers or farmers practicing small-scale agriculture. The earliest civilisation was the Minoan, from the island of Crete, which existed between 2200BC and 1450BC. The Mycenaeans were next, from mainland Greece and who famously engaged in the decade long siege of Troy. The Mycenaean age ended in about 1100BC and Hellas entered its Dark Age. In 800BC the Greeks started trading more with the outside world, they held the first Olympic Games and they fought the invading Persian army. This is known as the Archaic period. Around 480BC we arrive in Classical Greece, the golden age that lasted 200 years. In this period scientific discoveries happened, great plays were written, democracy was birthed and temples and art flourished. The final period between 323BC and 30BC is known as the Hellenistic period when the Romans took control. Rome didn't destroy the Greek way of life, rather, they respected it, copying many aspects of Greek culture and spreading Roman-Hellenic culture across the Mediterranean and beyond.

Greek Religion

I do not believe Greek mythology is Greek religion, although they are closely linked, the huge range of myths concerned with Gods, heroes and rituals embody the worldview of the ancient Hellenes after all. Many of us understand that the myths varied over time and any writer could change a myth, there are often several versions of the same story. They are a guide, but I wouldn't advise taking them literally, writers often change the roles played by their characters and therefore the overall message of the same myth can be different depending on the writer and indeed the audience it was intended for. Hesiod seems to have occasionally invented family links over several generations of deity to explain the origin and condition of the universe. The word *story* seems to be synonymous with Myth in Hellenic Pagan circles, they're for entertainment purposes and perhaps to try to explain the way the world worked to common folk. For a people so religiously minded, ancient Hellenes didn't have a word that means religion. The nearest terms were eusebeia meaning piety or devotion and threskeia meaning cult.

It's fair to say that the Hellenes had a way of life rather than a separate religious life and that in itself is what drew me personally to Hellenic Paganism. Historians tell us that this way of life can probably be traced back to before recorded time in one way or another. The practices we are aware of today seem to have lasted for more than a thousand years, starting around Homer's time, which is thought to be somewhere in the 8th or 9th century BCE, to the reign of emperor Julian in the 4th Century BCE.

As part of any path that attempts to revitalise and modernise an ancient way of life, I strongly advocate for the study of that history, to do that is a good place to start! Becoming acquainted with the history of those who were involved in it, together with their ethical, political, and intellectual experiences helps to give some context why things were done the way they were.

Just as modern-day Hellenic Paganism is a mingling of religious beliefs, it's thought Greek religion as we understand it now was a mix of the practices and beliefs between incoming people who arrived in Hellas from the north during the 2nd century BCE and the indigenous people whom they called Pelasgi. It's believed that these incoming folks brought with them a pantheon headed by an Indo-European sky god we now know as Zeus. It's likely there would have been a Cretan sky god, who was honoured with rituals and myths. The incomers would have applied the name Zeus to this Cretan counterpart and then at some point the deities would have been identified with local heroes and heroines from the Homeric poems to get such epithets, for example, as Zeus Agamemmon.

There's a school of thought that believes Homer and Hesiod gave the deities their home on Mount Olympus and once in that prestigious position they became identified with local deities. They would also have been made consorts of local deities, Zeus for example is said to have come to the Greek world with a consort but took Hera, a major goddess in Argos, as another, becoming polygamous, but uniting older and newer beliefs. An early form of integration if you like.

Some scholars believe that the Pelasgian and Greek parts of the religion can be untangled, suggesting that any fertility belief must be Pelasgian, on the grounds that the Pelasgi were farmers while the pastoralist nomadic warrior Greeks didn't have a pastoral requirement. I think this is quite simplistic, since pastoralists and warriors certainly need fertility in their herds, not to mention being fertile themselves.

What is Hellenic Paganism?

Something that draws a lot of people to Hellenic Paganism is the belief in many deities who are described by existing texts as having a human form or human attributes under a father-figure all-powerful God (Lord Zeus). To my mind this harks to

4

the Christian way of thinking - one must rule all - so I think for people rejecting mainstream religion, this is a way that makes some sort of sense. On a personal note, I may offer my respects to Zeus but I do not honour him as much as I do others; I came to this path via Goddesses, so in actual fact I think it's more about personal choice or as some have described it "a calling".

The sole requirement in ancient times and nowadays is to believe that the Theoi exist. It has been suggested that in ancient times to deny the existence of a deity was to risk reprisals from the deity themselves or their mortal followers, although contrary to that others believe if a Greek went through the motions of piety, he risked little, since there wasn't such a thing as an enforced orthodoxy. Devotion to the Theoi just happened. Hellenism is more about connecting with and understanding the relationship you have to the natural world, it is all about living the best life you possibly can, with virtue, rather than sin, punishment and redemption.

The simplest form of offering the Theoi piety is to perform acts of devotion which include ritual and sacrifice, of course sacrifice has changed a bit since ancient times, we'll come on to that later on. I've very much taken on the idea of praying to the Theoi, not merely to relevant deity either, but to any deity whose aid I have established through devotion which seems to have been the ancient Hellenes philosophy.

As far as we know there was no sacred text or clergy to speak of, priests would oversee cults, sacred sites and temples. In that respect not much has a changed, there are no sacred texts even modern ones, on the practices of ancient Hellenes. There are some very good books out there that I'll make reference too and I encourage you to get your hands on.

What we do know is that Greece was made up of difference polis (city states), and each polis had a series of public festivals throughout the year that asked the Theoi for their aid, for example, in matters like agricultural or warfare. This means that within the surviving writings there are a wealth of different festivals for the modern Hellenic Pagans to get their teeth into. My fellow Kitchen Witch coven members often comment that one of the reasons I am Hellenic is because of all the festivities!

We'll explore festivals in more depth, but, as a general introduction, there was and is, or should be, a social aspect, I enjoy the open rituals held by local groups as much as I do my own personal rituals at home. I long for a time lost when they attracted large gatherings (panegyreis). Mainly agricultural in nature, they were seasonal in character, held often at the full moon and on the 7th of the month in the case of Apollon and always with a sacrifice in full view of the attendees.

Many festivals were older than the deity they honoured. This notion reminds me of the modern concept of the Wheel of the Year and how the Celtic agricultural calendar is honoured now. Many Hellenic Pagans will have tried to adapt a Hellenic calendar to the Wheel of the Year to celebrate in line with their Pagan counterparts. I've tried myself and I'll share that journey with you a bit later.

Some festivals in Athens, where most of our information survives, were performed on behalf of the entire polis and all who resided within it. A lot of them were originally the cults of noble families who would come together at the synoikismos, the creation of the polis of Athens from its small towns and villages.

In the country, ways of life flourished around the worship of the omnipresent deities of the countryside, like the Arcadian goat-god Pan, who brought prosperity in flocks, or the nymphs who aided women in childbirth, inhabited caves, springs (Naiads), trees (Dryads and Hamadryads) and the sea (Nereids). They also believed in nature spirits such as the Satyrs, Sileni and Centaurs. As with other Pagan paths, nature is very important to the Hellenic Pagan. The waxing and waning of the seasons and the agricultural year feature really strongly throughout. Remembering this was survival to ancient people.

Magic was widespread. Spells were inscribed in lead tablets; wax dolls were created and petitions were made of deity. Statues of Hekate stood outside dwellings while Pan's image is said to have been beaten with herbs in times of meat shortage. As a witch myself, I've spent hours poring over extracts of magical papyri and researching ancient magic and then combining it with modern day tools to create my own magical practice with one foot in the 21st Century and one in the past.

Having no creed, Greek religion didn't recruit, in the heyday of city states such as Athens it was spread by the founding of new poleis who took with them a part of the sacred hearth fire from the mother city and the cults of the city's gods. I see every time I share some wisdom from my path as sharing a part of my hearth fire. This I gift to anyone who is willing to read on.

As with many paths there is no definitive right or wrong on how you choose to walk your path, but the spirit of piety remains strong. I will introduce you to arete (living to one's full potential) which embodies ethical frameworks of the Hellenic Pagan.

Who is the modern Hellenic Pagan?

The typical modern Hellenic Pagan is a curious, passionate, spiritual, hospitable person with their head stuck in a book who actively lives the path, practicing with devotion and the upmost respect for the Greek way of thinking, living and honouring the Gods. Personally, I am in love with Greece and her people, culture and philosophies.

There are Reconstructionists (people who attempt the daunting task of reconstructing an ancient way of living) and Revivalists (Hellenism as a living religion that changes with time). There are soft and hard polytheists, and those simply interested in honouring the Greek Gods. There are those who come across a Greek God in meditation and those that mix it up and work with many pantheons that happen to include Hellenic deities. There are heathens and witches, folk of Greek heritage, some without a drop of Hellenic blood in them and everything in between. Some Hellenic practitioners do not identify as Pagan, some consider the term derogatory, but personally I resonate with the term Hellenic Pagan, but those who don't, prefer the term Hellenic Polytheist. Others consider themselves as followers of Dodekatheism or Olympianism.

There are also followers of Hellenismos (a religion). I have an understanding of the principles and practices of Hellenismos, and although it doesn't make up my practice it has certainly helped in informing the way I practice. Somewhat similar, perhaps, to how a witch might have found Wicca to begin with. The term Hellenismos was coined by the Emperor Julian in the 4th Century AD.

Hellenism or Hellenismos in its current and ever-changing form came about in the 1990s, and split into two. Traditional Hellenismos and Reformed Hellenismos. Traditional is about following the spirit of ancient practice – understanding and knowledge of the ancient world is paramount; the Reformed is more of an eclectic form of worship.

An act of Kharis or Charis

"...the essence of Kharis is that the god is offered something pleasing. The worshiper establishes with a god a relationship not of strict indebtedness but rather one where the god remembers the gift and feels well-disposed in the future." (Pulleyn, p.87, 1997)

Here I open my arms wide as the Hellenes have done throughout time and invite you to continue the journey with me as I explore Deity and Myth and Living the Path.

I consider this work an act of kharis to the Greek Pantheon.

Part 2 – Living the Path

So, the one thing I get asked all the time, is how did I find myself wandering this path and how do I do it? First of all, I am still very much learning, so I cannot presume to know it all, and neither should anyone else. Also, let me clarify, I am a witch and Hellenic Pagan, if you are looking for subject matter on Hellenismos, although I will touch on it, there are some brilliant texts out there to get your teeth into.

If you want to learn some more about the Gods themselves, I talk about them in Part 3, and to be honest that's probably the best place to start if you've been hiding under a rock and never come across the Theoi at all, but if you've arrived here with a knowledge of the Gods already and you want to get down to the nitty gritty of worship, well this is where I started...

To be honest I thought I had a good handle on the Gods, until simple things like, "wait, the Hellenics call them Theoi" happened, or "wait, there are numerous versions of each mythology out there by different writers at different times." There again, what I actually began with was "OK, I'm floating along, kind of following the wheel of the year, and kind of trying to apply the gods I'm interested in to a Celtic system..." No wonder, then, that I wasn't feeling connected.

I was particularly interested in one myth, the story that encompasses how the seasons change, I couldn't get to grips with the wheel of the year system of god and goddess falling in love, getting pregnant, dying, ivy and holly battling it out against one another... but the story of Persephone's abduction and eventual return made sense to me. So, unlike many Hellenic Pagans, I feel like I stepped into this through the backdoor, through the Eleusinian Mysteries. Of course, as you'll see later on, there's not a lot to be found out about the mysteries and I felt like I was missing something, so upon typing such things into Google like the phrase "Greek Paganism", I came across Hellenism, and then Hellenic Polytheism and not long after that Hellenismos.

Feeling overwhelmed I finally found the website Hellenion where an article simply written by someone called Nicole M stated "Ours in primarily a devotional or votive religion, based on the exchange of gifts (offerings) for the god's blessings. Hellenismos has a highly developed ethical system based on the principles of reciprocity, hospitality, and moderation." (My Hellenismos 101, Nicole M, Hellenion.org) Reading this simple and clear article changed my life.

Ethics

According to Hellenismos there are seven Pillars which make up the ethical and moral framework of the religion, they are:

Arete – the practice of habitual excellence
Eusebia – reverence, loyalty, a sense of duty toward the gods
   of Greece
Hagneia – Maintaining ritual purity by avoiding miasma
Nomos Arkhaios – observance of ancient tradition
Sophia – the pursuit of wisdom, understanding and truth
Sophrosune – the control of self through deep contemplation
Xenia – adherence to hospitality

I believe many of them happen naturally like the second, fifth and sixth with practice and a touch of that scary notion known as discipline.

There's a word in there that seems to strike fear into a lot of new people wandering this path and that is "miasma" with regards to achieving the third Pillar. Also known as pollution, miasma refers to something like an aura of uncleanliness a person or space might attract/pick up through living and the idea of avoiding it is more about purifying self and space of it before contact is made with the Gods. The second part is really important. Everyone has their own ideas on what miasma actually is, to me it's not necessarily a negative thing, although the things that create it are sometimes linked to negative things, but more it's a part of being human and I believe the Gods understand that.

Things like death, sickness, birth, sex, excessive negative emotions and bodily fluids are included in creating miasma, as well as a lack of honouring the gods. These things create distraction, our minds are elsewhere when we're unwell or affected by life events. However, these things cannot be avoided and quite frankly certainly in terms of birth and sex shouldn't be avoided! Take care of yourself please, certainly in terms of mental and physical health, purify the space and self, to do this, make up a batch of khernips - use spring water, or boiled tap water and make it sacred by extinguishing a burning herb of your choice in the water (traditionally rosemary), it works as a form of Holy water, I make a new batch every new moon for the month ahead, we sprinkle some of the altar and wash our face and hands before ritual, in an act of purification of the pollution we pick up in everyday life. Enter into ritual/communion with the Gods your best self (Arete) and focus upon them and the rites you're going to perform.

I've mentioned that I have worked in Mental Health, I will admit that I've come home with the problems of the day on my mind, this to me is creating miasma, it's not like I won't approach the gods but I will spend some time getting mentally clear through meditation, talking to someone about it and how I'm feeling and then I will wash at the very least my hands and my face in khernips before I approach them in a formal way through ritual.

Arete is hugely important, and worth exploring further - I believe excellence is one of those terms that scares the pants off of people and although I'd like to believe I can be practically perfect in every way I am also very much a human being with very human flaws. So, for me, Arete is more akin to living the best I can, to my full potential. A system that supports this is found within the Delphic Maxims.

The Delphic Maxims

Apollon is said to have communicated the Delphic Maxims to Pythia, words of wisdom for living a good life, possibly originally from Zeus. These are thought to be the instructions for keeping out of Tartarus (the deepest part of Hades/The Underworld). An alternative explanation of their origin, however, is offered by Stobaeus, who attributed them to Seven Sages, or wise men of around the 6th Century. Perhaps they came about as many of these old folk sayings do in kitchens and over fences, and have been etched in stone for no other reason than the ancient form of graffiti. There are 147 Maxims to be exact, inscribed on the walls of the temple of Apollon. I encourage anyone wandering on to this path to look them up. I know some folk consider them the guidelines by which Hellenic Pagans live. Similar to the Witches Rede or Rule of Three.

The most famous Maxim wisdom in line with Arete is "Know thyself". As a devotional act to Apollon's gift of truth and knowledge I have this tattooed on my right shoulder. It's a really powerful and sometimes daunting piece of wisdom. I take it seriously, as do a lot of my fellow Hellenic pagans. When you do, you start to break through all of the misconceptions you have about yourself and others. You delve into who you really are and are meant to be. If done in conjunction with your own intuition and further guidance from the Theoi and/or the Universe it's my experience that you begin to make decisions that can be life altering, either bringing harmony or (as we know we cannot exactly control the divine) the revelation of big mistakes which often become opportunities to learn.

Other Maxims are more akin to the culture at the time they were supposedly brought to earth "Rule your wife", for example, and some don't really make a lot of sense at all like "Beget from noble routes." The former is cast aside and the latter is simply baffling. Other virtues which form Hellenism's ethical code include moderation, reciprocity, and self-control, all of which can be found in such texts as the Ten Tenets of Solon which include such things as "Do not speak falsely" and "When giving advice, do not recommend what is most pleasing but what is most useful".

The Golden Verses of Pythagorus, are a collection of sayings attributed to the Greek philosopher and mathematician and his followers that embody what we know about his teachings today for example "Sacred nature reveals to them the most hidden mysteries".

Finally, Aristotle's Ethics; Aristotle wrote two ethical treatises that begin with exploring eudaimonia (happiness, flourishing) and turn to an examination of the nature of Arete and the character traits that human beings need in order to live life at its best. Both explore the nature of pleasure and friendship and near the end is a discussion of the proper relationship between human beings and the divine. They're worth reading if you wish to gain an understanding of the ethics that underpin Hellenism.

The Hellenic Festival Year

The most complete calendars we have come from the Athenians. There are a few hints of festivals from other regions, but most Hellenists will use something like the Athenian Civil Calendar, shortened to the Attic here for ease, as a basis for their practice. It's also worth having a knowledge of Hesiod's auspicious days which can be found in his Works and Days, they set out what things should or should not be done in a month on individual days, making this practice literally a daily practice if you wish to follow it strictly of course.

Some might decide that the Attic is not authentic because Greece was made up of many city states with many different calendars. Even the Athenians themselves, especially from the 3rd century BCE forward, could consult five separate calendars, the Olympiad, Seasonal, Civil, Conciliar and Metonic. But the Athenian Civil calendar is the one you want to concentrate on, the one I tend to work with, and for your benefit when researching, it's also known as the Civil Festival Calendar.

All Athenian calendars use lunar cycles or solar events like equinoxes and solstices to plot out dates, the year roughly runs from midsummer to midsummer, whilst the days themselves are sunset to sunset. The calendar includes 12 to 13 months, named after the main festival of that month, the length varies because a lunar cycle calendar will slowly but surely drop behind a solar one. Once every three or so years the Athenians simply add an extra month when they needed to realign. In fact, you might see the phrase 'lunisolar' in your own personal research. The months consist of 29-30 days. Like the year itself, the months are longer or shorter in order to stay aligned with the moon and with solar events. The weeks of the months are separated into three blocks of 9-10 days each, I like to think of this as the waxing, full and waning month.

The Months

It's worth noting that depending on who has translated the Attic Calendar will depend on how the months are spelt, one such month happens in June/July!

The first month of the year, the Hellenic New Year, is called Hekatombaion (July/August) and begins at the new moon after the Summer Solstice, to the Athenians this was the start of summer. The rest of the calendar follows as such with two more summer months, Metageitnion (August/September) and Boedromion (September/October).

Autumn months are Pyanopsion (October/November), Maimakterion (November/December) and Poseidon (November/December), with a second Poseidon included when needed.

14

The winter runs Gamelion (January/February), Anthestarian (February/March) and Elaphebolion (March/April) and finally the spring Mounikhion (April/May), Thargelion (May/June) and Skirophorion/Skiraphorion (June/July). Athens itself doesn't really have a winter and they use the terms dry and wet months, although Greece does have snowy regions.

Adapting Calendars

Many people come to Hellenic Paganism from more mainstream forms of Paganism, like Wicca, and, therefore, tend to follow the Wheel of the Year.

It's been my mission over the past two years to develop my practice to match the world around me and where my interests are. I've researched and celebrated an entire Hellenic year previously, as it is set out by Hellenion, it was exciting and exhausting in equal measure! I wrestled with a few of the ethics of Hellenismos for this before I began to see that my true loyalty/reverence and excellence to the Theoi lays in finding my heart's path, so, I've adapted and will share with you how…

First of all, in celebrating or reading about as many as I could. Others, I learned about through 'Baring the Aegis' a blog by Elani Temprance and I believe Robert Clarke co-creators of the Hellenic Polytheistic group Elaion, I choose to celebrate one festival from the Attic calendar each month, and more than likely it will have some sort of relationship to the Eleusinian Mysteries, this harks back to my fascination with nature/seasons/agriculture and how I found this path. They might also be related to something that feels familiar to me, like Valentine's Day, for example, which can be aligned with the sacred marriage of Zeus and Hera (Hieros Gamos or Theogamia) which falls in Gamelion (January/February).

It may be that you have a particular deity you're drawn too and want to do more around their worship, but the Attic calendar doesn't really honour them that much. Ares is a good example of this; as a God of war, I've struggled to find festivals dedicated to him, he was prayed too before battle but that seems to be pretty much it. Anyway, you might find yourself feeling a bit disengaged. I fell into this category for a while before I realised just how many festivals I connected too and how I could still honour the Theoi alongside ritual/festivals even when they couldn't be done.

Some Hellenic Pagans choose to spend much time and effort trying to find information regarding other city states, and others have created modern day festivals and mixed them into the calendar. You have to find what works for you, but also try to understand where these ideas come from. If you really want to get a handle on each festival individually, I would recommend reading "Festivals of the Athenians" by H.W. Parke. There is also useful information on websites such as Hellenion and Temenos, and blogs like 'Baring the Aegis'.

My Adaptations, Some ideas

To begin with I simply took a Wheel of the Year festival, for example Mabon, and celebrated it verbatim whilst also placing a Hellenic God/dess in there, in Mabon's case Demeter/Persephone, until I came across Imbolc and Lammas where replacing Bridget and Lugh with a Hellenic deity just seemed rude!

My next step was to look at the concepts involved in the Wheel of the Year and match them with appropriate gods or align them with similar festivals held around the same time. I want to share with you an example, of what I mean.

Since it's Hellenic and my calendar begins in the summer, let's go with Summer Solstice. Summer Solstice falls in June and is also known as Midsummer or Litha. The day is long, ruled by the Sun and the night is short, it's a time for the fae and the otherworld. I associate Litha with sun celebration first, but also abundance, virility and strength. I would therefore choose to honour the deities associated with these aspects i.e.

Eros, Aphrodite, Apollon, Helios, Pan, Dionysos, as well as local nymphs and spirits of the land, this last one I will do at each point on the calendar.

Lampteria was a festival held in Achaia, honouring Dionysos Lampter (torch bearing) or Dionysos Lampteros (of the torches). The only surviving information we have is that people would carry torches to the temple of Dionysos, leaving vases of wine throughout the city. It isn't usually celebrated around June, it doesn't really have a fixed date and is simply referenced in research, but I get a chthonic aspect here, like Hermes guiding souls. Hermes for me is associated with travel over the summer holidays with Dionysos heading up revelry and summer bonfires on the beach, therefore I might even choose to include Poseidon.

Hellenion points to a festival called Prometheia in the Attic which is closer to the actual Solstice itself and honours Prometheus bringing fire, races, games, competitions, feasts and festivities to mankind. The Summer Solstice is one of four times when the gates to Divinity are open, which makes it, therefore, a good time to divine, receiving messages from the Universe.

To bring this together, I will choose one or more ways to honour the Gods in the example above and then Skiraphorion/ Skirophorion which is the month of the Summer Solstice has a festival related to the Eleusinian Mysteries.

I celebrate Skiraphoria or The Skira/The Skiro somewhere in June or July, it's often marked as the 12th Skiraphorion in the Attic but was actually a three-day festival in ancient times starting with processions from both Athens and Eleusis to a sanctuary on the Eleusis road called Skiran. Therefore, although I cannot find a reference to the Eleusinian Mysteries, it is, in my opinion, definitely related.

This festival is one of the few festivals where the women of Athens were allowed to gather in public to honour Demeter and ask her blessing for the harvest, although, when you look a little deeper, you see many festivals often honoured several deities. The Skira is no different with celebrations in Athens also honouring Athena and Poseidon.

It is first and foremost a fertility festival, women would abstain from sexual intercourse, eating garlic to keep the men away. Offerings of piglets, cakes shaped like a phallus or a snake would be thrown into sacred caves, all of which are fertility symbols symbolising when Hades opened a chasm into the earth to abduct Persephone and accidentally swallowed Eubouleus' swineherd. For me celebrating the festivals linked to the Eleusinian Mysteries is a cornerstone of my personal practice, plus summer solstice will always scream fertility to me. My hope is that this example gives you an idea of how you might adapt Hellenic festivals into a Wheel of the Year framework if you choose not to follow the Attic Calendar strictly.

The Sacred Month, Deipnon, Noumenia and Agathos Daimon

The sacred month begins at the first sliver of the moon also known as Noumenia, with "Old and New" (Hene Kai Nea or Hekate's Deipnon) celebrated the day after the new moon. Most witches celebrate (when there's still no visible moon in the sky), Noumenia the day the moon is first visible and Agathos daimon celebrated the day after that. This is something to get used to, it's taken everything for me to understand this, and I still struggle with it! It's made complicated by the fact the celebrations occur after sunset. Thankfully, Hellenion's downloadable calendar and Facebook page can help to navigate. I celebrate in the evenings, roughly around sunset or dinner time in the summer when the evenings take longer to draw in, so I will note when the new moon is occurring specifically on moon phase calendars local to my area, then plan to hold my Deipnon celebrations on whatever sunset is closest to the exact time and then follow suit with the other celebrations at the following sunsets.

The Deipnon

The Deipnon is dedicated to Hekate, it is the time to end the month and prepare for a new one ahead. It's thought that in ancient Hellas it was celebrated with a supper dedicated to the Titan Hekate, which was made up of onions, garlic, leek, egg, fish, bread (omelette is my go too) and cake (I make a honey cake). The meal was set at an outside shrine to Hekate and then placed at the crossroads as an offering to Hekate Trioditis (of the crossroads) and the vengeful spirits in her entourage.

The Deipnon is also about purification, apologises to my animal loving readers here, but it's thought a dog (Hekate's sacred animal) was taken in by the family, touched by everyone to transfer any negativity or miasma to it and then sacrificed by burning. I wouldn't have thought this was a monthly occurrence, perhaps when the family were particularly troubled and when the oikos (home) needed to keep or gain some favour with the Titan Goddess. Debts were often repaid at this time of the month; any unsettled business was completed, and the home was cleansed completely.

I'm used to preparing during the day (before sunset) and then having my ritual, but as the ritual is at sunset or thereabout, I end up doing the practical things the following day and the ritual first. The only thing I do before is cleanse, home and self. Part of the offerings made at the Deipnon are the sweepings from the home, which are offered to Hekate alongside a supper in her honour. If this occurs over a weekend, I will have done a clean of my entire home, and I am more likely to have hoovered up my sweepings during cleaning. I'm not a fan of rummaging through the bin or collecting the dust, hair and other nasties from the vacuum cleaner, so to get around this before the ritual I will at least have swept off my shrines and kept that and emptied my Kathiskos (see Noumenia).

I have a flame proof container that I fill with "sacrifices" I've made throughout the month, these are NOT perishable food items, I'll come back to disposing of food items when we talk ritual in more detail. These sacrifices are more like herbs, the ash from incense, spent charcoal discs, the barley traditionally used to cleanse a space, the ends of candles that haven't quite disappeared and any dust. more than likely I would have gathered them each day from my daily practice, so my container is pretty full.

It's fine if it's not a daily occurrence, by the way, your altar will still gather bits and pieces throughout the month regardless of whether you use it daily and a shrine that remains fixed will undoubtedly gather dust.

If it's been a particularly troubling month for my household, I will have crafted a small dog out of wax. At sunset, I will set my garlicy oniony omelette at my shrine to Hekate reciting Orphic Hymn 1 (or 0) to her. I will then take my container of sacrifices and add any sweepings from my altars. I will have more than likely had a bath or shower before I began but it's still important to cleanse with khernips, throw some cleansing barely into the container along with some ethanol and the wax dog (if using). Whilst again reciting the orphic hymn to Hekate I will light the ethanol in the container using a flame from Hestia's candle.

Throwing your windows open, staying with the burning, removing anything else flammable, having something to hand to douse the flames if it becomes out of control are vital... STAY SAFE! If you can do this outside in a fire pit even better.

Once everything is cooled, I can take the supper, burned offerings, undiluted wine and a mix of special herbs I make outside. I live in an apartment with a strip of wood behind me, which acts as my crossroads. Note that nothing must come back inside with you, including the plate with the meal on. Some have suggested banana leaves, but I like the idea of a tortilla or flat bread as suggested by Bekah Evie Bel, on her blog 'Hearth Witch Down Under' on Patheos, she mentions it several times in different articles when talking about leaving offerings outside.

At this point on the spot I will pray to Hekate to take any unwanted thoughts, habits, things I'd like to let go etc. I pour the entire glass of wine and then turn and leave without looking back. It's important to not look back, in case you get a look at the vengeful spirits and they follow you back inside!

The following day when the astronomical new moon would occur I will "pay off any debts", return any favours to friends or family, I will do one of those big jobs that always seem to get put off, like clean the cupboards out or do some odd jobs if it's not a working day. On a working day I tend to spend the day giving thanks for the blessings of the month and thinking about goals for the month ahead.

That evening once the sun has set, I will light a candle to Selene and offer her a hymn and some prayers, again thinking about the goals for the month ahead. As the personification of the moon this feels like the best time to honour her, at this point the first sliver of the moon will be visible in the sky so we're moving toward Noumenia.

The Noumenia

Noumenia is held in honour of the household gods, this day seeks blessings for the household, today is made for more honey cake! Usually the household gods consist of Hestia first and foremost, Hermes, Zeus Kthesios, Apollon Agyieus, and the Agathos Daimon. However, many Hellenic Pagans honour a plethora of deities in their households.

In the morning I offer a hymn, there are so many hymns, personally I love the Orphic and Homeric and there are some very good translations out there, and some sort of sacrifice to the deities I consider my household deities. At some point, depending on my schedule, I will refresh any seasonal decorations in my home. I will cook up a storm, something special my husband loves, and I will write down my goals and projects for the month ahead, this might also include plotting out my ritual calendar.

I noted my Kadiskos above, this is the time I will refresh the ingredients in it. This "small bucket" is made in honour of Zeus Ktesios (protector of the household goods or he who cares for the prosperity of the household). The previous night I will have emptied and cleaned an old-fashioned sweet jar with a sealable lid, although traditionally a new jar is selected each month, I recommend mason jars which are fairly cheap and easy to source if you're going to create a new one each month. Personally, I don't agree with simply throwing something away when it can be used again after a thorough clean.

I say sealable because the contents of this jar will likely ferment or rot, therefore, if it doesn't seal you risk spoiling the very food you're trying to protect! So, take your cleaned-out jar and add a small amount of olive oil, add bits of food that the family has on hand, like a pinch of flour, seasonal fruit, rice, honey, herbs, maybe even some chocolate. "We put anything we find and ambrosia in it. Ambrosia is pure water and oil and all fruit..." Anticleidues (Hellenic Pagan Organisation Hellenion member)

Go with your intuition, if I have a particular goal or intent for the month ahead, I might adjust my offerings to match that, i.e. if I want to bring more love into my home, I will ask myself what ingredients stir up thoughts of love, usually that means adding some rose petals. Remember you're asking Zeus Ktesios to protect your wealth essentially, when emptying the jar, the night before I will give thanks for his protection, and as 'Baring the Aegis' suggests, I recite Orphic Hymn 14.

Fill the jar to the top with water, spring water or bottled water is less likely to go stale and smell as quickly as tap water, but I've not found much difference with tap water and some folk say ambrosia would be something like mead not spring water. Anyway, tightly seal the jar. Traditionally the containers would have "...thread white wool and yellow thread..." from Anticleidues. It's optional of course, I braid two white and one yellow strands of wool together and tie them around the lid. I've also braided different colours in there if I have a specific intent for the month with regard to my familial "wealth" I might choose green if I'm trying to eat more veggies for example!

Traditionally this jar was kept in the pantry where food is stored, I'm a bit funny about rotting food being near fresh, even with a tightly sealed lid, so I place it on my kitchen shrine to Hestia.

Agathos Daimon

The Agathoi Diamones, meaning good spirits, are thought to be mediators between Gods and humans, making them a helpful kind of spirit but "One must be on good terms with it" (W. Burkert, Greek Religion, 2013, ebook. The name daimon does not mean evil like the term demon in modern Christianity, daimones do have both negative forms (Kakodaimon) and good forms (Eudaimon), we pray for a good one. They are thought to be an aspect of Zeus, as Ktesios, Charitodotes and Epikarpios all titles that speak of Zeus as a deity who brings joy and increases in all things good including honour and wealth.

Household spirits are often depicted as snakes, which is a sign of healing to Hellenic Pagans, or a young man with a golden horn of plenty symbolising, to my mind, abundance. I've meditated a lot on this and found my daimon to be in the form of a black serpent.

There's a school of thought which I tend to subscribe to myself that believes the daimon is a part of one's being. In Apology by Plato, Sokrates speaks of his own daimon as a small voice inside who guides him, warning him to not do certain things. I strongly believe my intuition takes the form of a snake; I can almost guarantee I will dream of a black snake when I have a decision to make. When I'm about to do something that goes against my intuition I will see or hear about a snake somewhere in my day to day.

Praying to the Agathos Daimon of your oikos or indeed yourself is often, in my opinion, the best way to communicate with this household spirit. Offering libations of unmixed red wine, an incense blend and a hymn of your choosing (Orphic 72 is a good one) on this sacred evening is the perfect nod and end to a very important three-day event to the Hellenic Pagan.

Of course, there will be many variations out there, I really love reading about how others celebrate, each of us has an interpretation of the sources we have read, I love that this path is so varied and full of interpretation. There are some guiding lights in the form of organisations who have laid down the basics like ritual formats and calendars and then the rest is up to the follower and the community.

Hesiod's Auspicious Days

I wanted to share Hesiod's auspicious days as set out in his piece Works and Days. His work, including the Theogony, accompanied by Homer's Illiad and Odyssey has shaped the way Hellenic Pagans view society in ancient Hellas.

I want to demonstrate how you can practice following the special days in a month where things should or should not be done. The thing to remember is that they don't always line up with modern life, or in fact the life outside of agriculture. Some of them make no sense whatsoever to the modern mind set.

I take note of the days that a deity is involved and choose to nod to them through burning some incense, and/or lighting a candle along with reciting a hymn or saying a prayer. On those where it says it's an "unkindly" day I tend to ask for a little more protection.

Day 1 – Sacred Day (Noumenia as discussed above)

Day 3 – The Tritogeneia, in honour of Athena

Day 4 – Sacred, good day to bring home a bride, good day to begin building narrow ships; open jars on this day – I like to think of this day as the day to begin building projects, a crafty or creative day. This is also a day to take care to avoid troubles that eat out the heart. I like to use some time on this day to concentrate on all that is good in my life.

Day 5 – Unkindly day which is sacred to Horcus (oath), the Eriynes (the Furies) and Eris (Strife) – I tend to carry a protection crystal on the 5th days of every month (5th, 15th, 25th) and I don't make promises to others on this day.

Day 7 – Sacred to Apollon, Artemis, and, Leto, I nod to Artemis and Apollon during the day and evening for their associations with the sun and moon. Leto is a motherly goddess so if I've not spoken to my mum for a few days, I make sure to contact her.

Day 8 – Good working day, good day to castrate boars and bulls. I nod to Hermes and/or Athena on working days for wisdom, strategy, money matters, support at work.

Day 9 – Good working day, and sacred to all the Gods, particularly the nine muses; this for me is a good day for inspiration, the arts and sciences.

Day 10 – Good for the birth of males.

Day 11 – Good working day – shearing sheep and reaping fruit, I ask myself if anything has come to fruition by this point in the month. The eleventh is sacred to the Moirai (the Fates), I like to meditate on my journey and divine for answers on the future.

Day 12 – Good working day – shearing sheep, reaping fruit, female works, castrating mules.

Day 13 – Best day for setting plants, good day to set out supplies; worst day to start sowing. This day is sacred to Athena for me and The Greek Magical Papyri speaks of honouring Selene.

Day 14 – Sacred day – good day for the birth of a female and good day for taming sheep, oxen, guard dogs and mules. Some consider the 14th sacred to all gods, the middle of the month and could be around the full moon.

Day 15 – Exactly like the 5th, extra protection needed on this day.

Day 16 – Good for the birth of males (although he might be fond of "sharp speech, lies and cunning words"), good day for castrating sheep and children, good day for fencing in a sheep cot; unfavourable for plants, bad for the birth of a female, bad day to get married.

Day 17 – Sacred to Demeter, throw down the grain on the threshing floor, good for cutting beams for houses and ships. It's a good day to be thankful for the food we have. Also sacred to Apollon.

Day 18 and 19 – attributed to lustral and apotropaic rituals as told by Philochorus. These days are sacred after noon and never an unkindly day.

Day 20 – Wise men should be born – I like to dive into learning something new today.

Day 21 – Sacred to Apollon

Day 24 – Better during the morning, less so towards the evening. I don't tend to worship after sunset on this day.

Day 25 – See 5th and 15th, yes, you guessed it, an unkindly day.

Day 26 – Sacred to Artemis

Day 27 – Good day for opening wine jars, putting yokes on oxen, mules and horses. Good day for bringing ships out of dry dock. Another day to avoid troubles that eat out the heart, it's a good day to get rid of thoughts, activities that make you suffer, especially since we are entering a sacred time at the end of the month.

Day 30 – The Deipnon, the holiest of days, for purification of home, affairs and soul.

Practice

Ancient authors often show a reluctance to share explicit details of religious ceremonies and rites, but what we do know is the common practices were processions, sacrifice (usually pig, sheep, goat or cows, though sometimes human) and the pouring of libations (liquid) out on the altar, which would have been outside of the temples (naos – meaning dwelling) that were eventually built to "house" or at least temporarily offer space to the gods, accompanied by prayer and hymns in their honour.

With a temple setting, or even the big complexes like the acropolis known as temenos or sanctuaries where there would have been monetary donations, dedicatory statues, fountains and other buildings there would be formal, big city rituals and special occasions. The Greeks would have had simple home shrines and altars as well.

Altars and Shrines

I know a lot of folk wish they had a temple they could visit, some organisations in America have opened some, if you're within touching distance... GO! I am lucky enough to be within a short plane ride of Greece herself, to visit at least, so I can't complain that I don't have a specific public space to attend in the UK.

I make do with my apartment and the various sacred spaces that surround me. The home altar and household worship are the cornerstones of my practice, and, like many others, I believe Hellenic Paganism wouldn't function without these spaces. For some extra reading on household worship I recommend "Hellenic Polytheism: Household Worship: Volume 1" written by Labrys members (Labrys are a group of Hellenic Polytheists based in Athens who are leading the way in reviving the ancient ways. This topic is hugely emotive in Greece, as a country with very strong religious values.) This differs from quite a lot of paths where there doesn't necessarily need to be a space to worship at, although I strongly believe the Gods' reside in every aspect of my life and can quite easily commune with Athena in my search for wisdom, say, at a library, but the spaces I create in my home are paramount.

As the members of Labrys share on the website (http://www.labrys.gr/en/), I see the altar as like a bridge to communicate with the Gods. Altars in ancient times seemed to be categorised depending on the type of offering i.e. sacrificial, fiery, non-fiery/bloodless and depending on the level they are to the ground, can be dedicated to Chthonic (of the earth), Olympian and altars of the dead (ancestor worship).

On reflection what I have set up in my home nods to identifying as a witch also - I have shrines and what I refer to as a working altar.

Practically speaking, in our modern world of space, and being mindful of other human beings we dwell with, (who in ancient times would have worshipped alongside us) a lot of us are solitary so, you can swap altars out when worshipping different deities, and go with your intuition in terms of who wouldn't mind sharing with who if you want to create more permanent spaces but are still limited on space in general. In days gone by, a recess, the central hearth of the home, or even an entire room may have been used for household worship, let alone the journey to the sanctuaries and altars of the village/town you lived in.

In terms of difference between shrines and working altars, my shrines are permanent spaces I have created that depict the gods I work with, they are a celebration of that deity. I have statues which have come from all manner of places (Etsy, Ebay, even Amazon and Greece herself) and when I haven't been able to afford a statue or find one I am happy with I use a picture I feel drawn to, in fact I love the written word accompanied by pictures, sometimes obscure quotes and pictures that hint at the symbols of the deities.

I believe the place where you honour the Gods is very personal. I always include at the very least a candle and somewhere to burn incense. They are my temples and are treated with as much loving care and attention as I would any sacred space inside or outside the home.

I see so many folks asking for ideas on what to include and so many offering suggestions. I don't have any mystical or historical suggestions for this, what I do is go on to the internet and type in "symbols and icons of (insert deity)", to get some ideas. I'll then grab my books and a notebook, read the myths and the hymns that are associated with that deity, noting down any specific symbols that come to mind as I immerse myself in the stories.

Then I go out and see if I can find, make, and/or acquire any. Charity shops/thrift stores are a gold mine as is the world around us, for example, a few years ago my husband and I had a holiday in Dorset; we went to one of my favourite little seaside towns where I had a platter of seafood for a romantic dinner on a balmy evening, delicious, romantic! The crab I was served came in a seashell that Lady Aphrodite is often depicted riding, particularly by Renaissance artists. I asked the waitress what they do with the seashells and she said they throw them away, so quite unashamedly I wrapped up the shell and brought it home. After a very thorough clean, that shell now sits on my shrine to the great lady of beauty and love, not only because you see her riding one in works of art but because that night was full of beauty and romance. Another example is a wedding I was blessed to be maid of honour at, I had a lovely small bouquet of artificial red and white roses and I've placed those on my space honoured to Lady Hera as the Goddess of marriage. Simple, yet meaningful.

I've had quite a lot of fun making things to go on my shrines, I've been a keen crafter for many years, I've made a crochet blanket in the colours of the flowers Kore was picking in the spring meadows, a moon phase wall hanging to honour Selene and an ivy and deep red rose crown to honour Dionysos. I had a go at sculpting using air drying clay before I found the aesthetic pictures. I strongly believe that the things we make in honour of deities carry something very special within them.

I don't see this as worshipping an idol, an image as such, what I see is a visual representation of the Gods themselves, somewhere to direct my worship instead. I also see these trinkets and treasures as offerings in themselves, gifts if you like. Therefore, I treat each and every part of my shrines as sacred objects, regularly purifying and cleansing them at appropriate times. When an item no longer has that "yes moment" I will dispose of it with care and attention, like I would any other type of offering.

Working Altar – Ritual Tools

My working altar is a different place altogether, central to my shrines, akin to the place outside of the temple where the actual worship happened in ancient times. After some research on rituals and customs which we'll come onto shortly I have built a working altar that includes as much of the ancient tools of worship as I can accomplish with the modern tools at my disposal. I long for an outside space where this could be accomplished, but I am adaptable and flexible in thought. There's some traditional thinking out there that states the altar dedicated to worship should somehow not be accessible to guests, and therefore should be curtained off or in a room where only the family may go.

These tools are dedicated to their use, I don't use them for anything else, I've spent time finding the right items for me and my worship, this act of dedicating for the purpose of worship feels like it induces a sort of mental state toward the acts themselves. When I say dedicating, there might be some really complicated rituals out there to do that, for me it's more about cleaning them, maybe passing them through some incense and although it sounds a little crazy, simply telling them their purpose from now on!

Candles – I don't have a hearth fire/fire place, which is central to household worship, I have a kitchen with a shelf dedicated to Hestia which holds a candle that represents my hearth fire, traditionally it should be lit all the time, but I'm barely home so I have an electronic candle that is "lit" all the time and a "hearth candle" I light when I'm preparing food generally and/or for ritual. I want the candles I use to be made of natural substances like beeswax, so quite often I will source natural/sustainable materials and make my own. This candle isn't part of my working altar. Some have oil lamps to represent their hearth fire, equally I would want to use a natural oil.

A glass bottle for khernips (purified water) with a pretty bowl wide enough to dip my fingers in and a white towel only used for drying my hands and face when I've cleansed with khernips.

Libation and offering bowls to receive various offerings (liquid and solids)

A small cast iron cauldron, I am a witch after all. This is the place I've chosen to put anything I burn, like pieces of paper/ food items etc, because I didn't trust my offering bowls to withstand the heat.

Incense holders, and a place to store incense and other offerings like barley or tools like charcoal.

A wine glass (which I fill with whatever liquid is needed at the time) this represents the clay pots you see – Amphoras.

A small bottle of olive oil (a common offering I make).

Ritual

Rituals need not be complicated, there are a wealth of amazing simple rituals out there for all kinds of things in broader Pagan terms, but there are very few rituals already written and available. But there is good news, there is a ritual format for the Hellenic Pagan. I'm not sure where it came from originally, but I can muse that the basic format came from reading snippets of information in such works as Hesiod's Works and Days, and the epic poems like that of Homer and other ancient writers. There's been a number of finds by archaeologists that help people understand what might have been happening in ancient times on a large city scale and books such as "Religions of the Ancient Greeks" by Simon Price and my personal favourite, Walter Burkert's "Greek Religion". Regardless of where modern Hellenism got its ritual format, I believe it's one of the most adaptable and friendly to work with.

> **Preparation** – This stage will include gathering everything you're going to need for your ritual, this might include cooking and/or baking for "feasting". For me, this stage will often include a bath or shower, some music and meditation that will get me into the present moment. I don't have ritual clothes, but I do like to be clean, neat and tidy. When it comes to ritual clothes, I've noticed Labrys who worship in Greece, tend to wear either white or red with flower and/or laurel crowns. Some people choose to veil during rituals or during prayer.

> **Procession** – In ancient times this would have been how the worshippers got everything to the temple site. I don't know if it was a household practice. I do process from my kitchen to my living room where my shrines and altars are.

> **Purification** – Most Hellenic Pagans will use Khernips to

purify, this is also known as lustral or holy water. I make a large batch on Noumenia to use throughout the month. You should use water that is purified, I tend to boil tap water or pass tap water through a filter. I just can't buy bottled water on a plastic, mother earth stance, but do what works for you. You pour the water into a bowl and then drop a flaming herb (I use Rosemary for purification) into it with a pinch of salt. You wash your hands and face by dipping your fingers into the bowl and sprinkling or dabbing the water on to yourself, I tend to then sprinkle a small amount on my altar. You then use a clean white towel to dry yourself. Barley is often used to purify as well. You scatter less than a handful on your altar. If you're particularly concerned about sprinkling barley, for example, if have curious animals or children, you could sprinkle some into an offering bowl.

The Ritual - The key elements to a ritual include lighting candles and lighting incense whilst reciting hymns to the deities you're honouring and other hymns that might be appropriate to the celebration, even writings you have written yourself. You then make offerings to the deities, if praying or requesting anything you do it during the offering. If it is an Ouranic ritual you can partake in any food that wasn't offered, but never eat anything in a Chthonic ritual and you must burn offerings made to the Chthonic deities. More hymns follow, as well as anything else you might have added. A note on magic – I am a witch and will add spells and workings here, but magic is not always considered appropriate within Hellenismos. As this path is more about honouring, gifting, praying, requesting and thanking, magic is sometimes seen as an effort to bend the will of a deity or the Universe. I think it depends on the ritual; at Deipnon I will do what I consider to be a modern releasing spell to move forward, for example.

You offer a libation next, it's worth checking whether the being to whom you are offering likes alcohol, this will be within the writings associated with the deity and/or festival; one example is the nymphs I've found prefer milk and honey. The libation can include more hymns/writings if you have them. Again, if it's an Ouranic ritual you can partake the remainder of the libation, during Chthonic you empty the contents completely. You finish by extinguishing the candles and saying farewell and thank you however you deem fit.

As you'll find out in Part 3 on building relationships with deities, Hellenic Pagans will honour Hestia first and last, by honouring her at the beginning and end of each ritual. She will also receive a portion of the offering and libation.

Personally, I don't cast/uncast a circle or call/dismiss the quarters as you would in most Wiccan rituals, as it's not a requirement of the Hellenic tradition. However, it is my opinion that if these parts of ritual are important to you, then you go ahead and slip it into your rituals at the appropriate points. My practice will differ from almost everyone I've come across, it's my creation of ancient practice as I understand it to be.

I will move (process) the candle from the shrine (temple) to the deity I'm honouring to my working altar, after having lit it from my already lit hearth candle on my kitchen altar. I will centre myself a moment asking silently that the deity join me for the working. I will light some incense at the shrine, because that is where my deity is dwelling and light the same incense on my working altar to create the bridge.

My reasons for having a more complex process is I do not have the space for a large altar with statues, symbols and trinkets as well as the working part of my practice and, as I've said before, I don't have a hearth fire, I see my kitchen as my hearth which is a separate room to my shrines/altar apart from my Hestia shine. of course.

Animal Sacrifice

It wouldn't be a book about Ancient Greece if I didn't talk about animal sacrifice, there seems to be a fair few misconceptions about this practice in the ancient world, so I'll start there. Today we have a lot of meat availability, whether that's ethical or not is neither here nor there for my purposes. In the ancient world, meat for food was not readily available, only the richest and most privileged of ancient Hellas would have had access to meat. It's said that the Greeks in general chose not to eat meat outside of sacrifice, believing that eating meat was barbaric. But killing for a God and then partaking in said sacrifice gives that death some kind of purpose.

What we now consider to be organic and free range as our best way of treating animals would have been the standard in times gone by, so imagine what their best treatment of an animal would have been... those were the animals selected for sacrifice.

Animal sacrifice was not as common as you might think, it was reserved for special occasions, there wasn't the livestock available to make daily sacrifices to each deity.

According to "An Overview of Classical Greek History from Mycenae to Alexander" by Thomas R Martin, the sacrifice itself was an elaborate affair, the animal had to have the very best treatment, with no harm from humans and only a small amount of hair taken for the fire, it would be decorated with flowers and led to the altar in such a way so as one would assume it had the choice, you can imagine someone laying down a trail of food. They would be blessed with water (perhaps khernips) so it would end up shaking its head as if saying "yes". Prayers of reverence would happen before its throat was slit by skilled people. The whole affair was solemn, women would scream as the animal died and music would play.

If you read how Prometheus ascertained which parts of the animal the Gods would consume, you will see that the parts given in sacrifice aren't necessarily the parts we as humans would eat. When those parts were given to the fires, the animal was butchered for food and shared out to the masses. The act of sacrifice was two-fold, it maintained Kharis (relationships) with the Gods but it also fed the community, some of which wouldn't get meat at any other time.

It's rare to find a Hellenic Pagan who will sacrifice animals, we simply do not have the skills, of course we could learn... but to be fair, there are all kinds of ethical, moral, and, legal restrictions which such a practice, and many are vegetarians and vegans. Also, the majority of us don't really know how our meat was truly raised. Some Hellenics will use meat they have brought, if they can guarantee the source.

For me, I create no meat alternatives, I've crafted animal shapes out of clay before now and set them upon my shrines as a permanent sacrifice. I will bake cookies in the shape of an animal so it's still a food offering that can be burnt. I've made cupcakes and decorated them to look like animals. When there are so many offerings out there in the form of fruits, flowers, hymns, song, dance, candles, liquid libations, herbs, cakes, cookies and incense, animal meat doesn't even factor in my sacrifices.

Offerings

Household worship was important to the Ancient Greeks, as it is now with modern Hellenics. Since we've established that animal sacrifice as offerings wasn't possibly in the everyday, we can summarise that offerings given outside of those special occasions, were probably a lot more accessible. Meaning, the modern-day Hellenic Pagan has a plethora of options.

Natural foods such as fruit and vegetables that are in season make excellent offerings. I tend to look for fruits and vegetables that are in season naturally at the time of year I am making my offerings. I use a seasonal food calendar to help me and when looking at the supermarket I try to find items that are produced in the UK. Which doesn't always measure up to traditional offerings but does connect me to the world around me.

Honey is important in offerings; it is considered the "nectar of the Gods" or ambrosia. The Greeks didn't have sugar. They would often sweeten their bitter wine with honey and a favourite of mine is to offer a Greek inspired honey cake. They considered honey as having powerful medical properties and it was used in various beauty products. I will use honey that is produced locally to me and is kind to our bees.

There are limitations with my seasonal offerings, the seasonal time for one of the most prolific offerings to a Hellenic Pagan, the humble grape, has a very short season in October in the UK, so what I do is find grapes that have been imported from Greece for special occasions. Grapes make wine, again incredibly sacred and one of the most traditional offerings you can make. I like to find local wines to offer the Gods as libations. On very special occasions I may source a Greek wine, but just like anything else imported I am conscious of my carbon footprint. It seems sweetening the wine with honey as mentioned above is another special occasion custom, the Greeks would, however, mix their wine with water, remember when Dionysus brought wine to the people, it was claimed in myth the people were blinded. Only when wine is offered to chthonic deities can wine be offered unmixed. Since we do not partake in anything offered in chthonic rites, we aren't likely to go blind!

Olives are known for their sacredness, we all know the story of how Athena and Poseidon fought over Athens, to win the battle for patronage Athena created the Olive tree. The olive, like honey, is versatile enough to be baked into breads and the oil is sometimes used in cakes. Olive oil is also a fuel and can be used to power oil lamps and if you don't have any wine but you do have olive oil, it makes a wonderful libation.

Fish seems to have been a staple of the Mediterranean diet, and why not with those fantastic coastlines. Today we consider fish a meat product, but I can't imagine ancient people's running live fish from the harbour to the altar to be sacrificed, so it seems they are considered something different.

Personally, the only source of fish I have is frozen or canned, which for me doesn't feel right, but I've heard of other Hellenics who fish regularly and therefore do make fish offerings to the deities. Poseidon is an obvious choice, as are other water deities and records show Hekate received red mullet on the Deipnon.

I mentioned barley when I was talking about purifying the altar in ritual. Barley was incredibly important to the ancient Greeks as it was their main crop and source of food. Because of its purifying properties I like to try to use local barley flour in ritual baking. It's fair to say that understanding the deities you are worshipping is the first step before making offerings, you will find in myth that there are some offerings that are more important to some and not others.

One thing I enjoy doing is finding recipes online that include some of these traditional offerings, I enjoy cooking and since we get to partake in the offerings we make to most Gods, I love to cook up a feast to enjoy as part of special occasions.

There are other offerings that can be offered alongside food, I like to offer flowers, for example, and I also go out into the world around me and find leaves, twigs, berries (when they're in season). Permanent offerings such as the clay animals I mentioned earlier, but also things like coins, jewellery can be worn in honour or placed on the shrine. Some will offer gemstones, stones and shells from the beach, feathers found on your path. I do have a skull on my chthonic altar which was sourced from a friend who processes roadkill into decorations. Some of these things can be offered through burning, burying or leaving out for nature to reclaim, especially when flowers wilt or the leaves dry. Unless of course I'm going to use them in magic... yes, still a witch!

One of the simplest offerings is incense. We don't all have time to make loose incense, although it's preferable, I do often burn sticks and cones to the Gods. If you seriously don't have anything else to offer, incense is the absolute go too. I like to check with the Orphic Hymns for incense offerings to specific deities, you might see the term aromatics, I can't find what that means, so I tend to make an offering a nice smelling one. Frankincense is the most common offering, with supplies of frankincense in the world being as they are, and unethical harvesting, I personally only use frankincense for special occasions.

I'm all for doing things that make sense to you, do a little research, of course, but equally go with what calls you. Chocolate and sweets are a classic example of this, I've noticed a lot of people will offer sweets to Hermes and chocolate to Aphrodite. I've been known to offer watered down liquor to Ares for no other reason than as a God of battle, I associate whiskey with soldiers I have known.

Keep in mind who you are offering too, is it an Ouranic or a Chthonic offering? Ouranic is always partial, you may partake, chthonic is complete, you may not. Which can be a little tricky when we're talking bread for example, you wouldn't want to offer an entire loaf to Hades, what a waste. I tend to offer an entire slice of bread! I believe it's entirely up to you to decide what is an offering in its entirety.

The act of actually making the offerings can include; consumption entirely by fire which is traditional, referring back to one of my favourite bloggers, Elani of 'Baring the Aegis' suggests putting safe ethanol in to a fire proof bowl, dropping the offering in and then extinguishing the fire with the libation. Burying it is more of an option for the chthonic. Using offering bowls (which tends to be what I use for lack of safe fires and outside space as we talked about earlier).

I hear a lot of talk about how to dispose of offerings, especially when you don't have access to a garden, which I don't. I've mentioned before I'm lucky to live in front of a wooded area where I can dispose of most offerings, but I'm not able to bury anything and food offerings left out would attract some unwelcome creatures. But I have other options. My workplace has a compost bin, for example, or a friend my take it for their compost bin. There's some contention over throwing it away into the bin, now I don't condone simply tossing it into the rest of the trash, that would be disrespectful, however, and I say this because failing leaving it to nature or giving to a friend I have as a last resort disposed of the offering in a bin. My reasoning is that if the offering has been left for a time on the shrine/altar and I feel that deity has had their fill, then that offering to me is no longer 100% sacred. I will treat it better than simply tossing it away with the rest of the trash, however. I will wrap it in tissue, and bind it closed with a compostable material before placing it in the bin, often whispering an apology.

Part 3 – Relationship with Deity

Although I believe ritual and acts of devotion to be a cornerstone of this path, they wouldn't occur without the Gods and beings they honour. I have chosen the Theoi out of all of the other pantheons, but I'm not above entertaining those from other religions, I am a hard polytheist after all, I believe all Gods from all religions exist.

I choose to honour the Theoi through deep personal experience. When I say personal experience, I mean signs in nature, messages while meditating, things I've read, seen, heard or tasted that speak to my heart, feelings of intuition, events that keep happening. It's like a heart calling, a vibration somewhere deep in the soul. A lot of Pagans refer to this as the Universe speaking, as a Hellenist, it's the Theoi, usually shouting and looking a lot like that guardian angel meme on social media with her head in her hands.

The last I experienced was an urge to go to the sea, as I sat there with the sun on my face (unusual for December in the UK) on Winter Solstice morning I had a feeling I needed to write down things that I wanted to let go of in the sand for the waves to wash it away – a cleansing so to speak. It was only when I reflected afterwards that I realised fully it was the month of Poseidon on the Attic Calendar and the festival of Posidea. I didn't plan it at all. I was celebrating Winter Solstice with fellow witches at Stonehenge welcoming Helios back from the Underworld when I had a deep desire to go to the sea - to honour Lords Poseidon and Helios together.

I hope it will become more apparent as we move forward together, that when you listen, notice, and crucially, act - your relationship with your path and your Gods deepen, this brings you closer to your Pantheon.

Get to know your Pantheon

I've been doing a 30-Day Deity Devotional Challenge. Each month I choose a being I will get to know by pulling a card from one of my favourite decks: *Mythic Oracle: Wisdom of the Ancient Greek Pantheon* by Carisa Mellado. Each day I research and write about them. I've been doing it for two years now and have three precious notebooks full of research, thoughts and personal experience. When I've completed all the beings depicted in the deck, I will have touched only a small portion of the Pantheon. There are thousands of creatures, heroes, daimones (spirits), and of course Gods in the Greek pantheon because quite simply the people of the ancient world believed the Gods are in everything.

I'm not going to reinvent the wheel in this section by talking too much about all of the individual Gods, I want to do them justice with introductions to those I see as imperative, for now though there are some amazing books and websites out there that are worth having in your arsenal of resources, *"The Gods of the Geeks"*, C. Kerényi, is one of my favourite books as recommended by Sarah Kate Istra Winter in her book *"Kharis: Hellenic Polytheism Explored"* (another must have on the Hellenic Pagan book shelf) and the website theoi.com is a true treasure trove of all things Greek Pantheon, the internet is an absolute joy for researching, getting others opinions and ideas and generally connecting with information, a modern day library of Alexandria!

Read. Learn. Observe. Read everything you can get your hands on to do with your Gods, with an air of caution that they are written by human beings with their own thoughts, beliefs and understandings.

Connecting with others

Speaking of this thing called the Internet. I believe it has afforded us the ability to connect with many more people worldwide, as well as some interesting pitfalls I'm not here to talk to you about other than be safe and walk away if it doesn't feel/look right, I have discovered one huge benefit - I'm subscribed to a few different YouTube channels, blogs and I'm a member of different groups/pages on social media.

Videos and pictures shared of Hellenics coming together as a group and people who are out there actively engaging in this path, offering support, guidance, opinion and interesting insights to others has been inspiring and validating. I know there are folks out there that think they know it all and seem to think they have some sort of authority over others. I also know there are a large proportion of folk out there just wanting to connect, learn and share their experiences. Those places are the places where gold mines of information thrive and believe it not, even the local know it all will have valuable information to share.

The ancient Greeks worshipped publicly as we've talked about. These community rituals were paramount to culture in Ancient Greece, honouring the Gods in a very public forum was just a way of life and great importance. When the belief was that if you didn't honour Demeter, your crops might fail and your community might starve, then you can see why practicing on a large scale was important.

I often find myself at home doing a ritual and imagining what it would be like if my entire community were doing the same things as me. Processing through my living room and gorging myself on a feast doesn't always have the same ring to it. Since we don't have a lot of surviving anecdotes or evidence of household practice, I was craving connecting with others to deepen my relationship with the Theoi.

That's where I came across 'Baring the Aegis' a blog and an associated Facebook group called Elaion. The Hellenics responsible for these gems have created something called PAT or "Practice at Home" a really simple idea which I'm sure isn't unique to them but it is genius in my eyes. They create events based on the Attic Calendar; they provide ritual outlines you can download and research regarding the festivals. So even though I am not in Greece or in America where a lot of Hellenes seem to be, I do feel closer to the Theoi because I am part of a community worshipping them together.

I'm also a member of an incredibly supportive Coven who join me in the occasional Hellenic inspired ritual online and in person. I am incredibly grateful for these individuals and the group as a whole for their curiosity about my chosen path which often leads to cake, lots of laughter and the occasional exploding offering dish.

The ancients worshipped and celebrated together publicly. Consider connecting with others.

Open your mind

A lot of us come to Hellenic Paganism with some basic knowledge of the Gods of Olympus, childhood story books, history class and those black and white films from yesteryear. Before I stepped on to the path of a Hellenic Pagan, I was quite happy with a basic understanding of the Big Twelve, Aphrodite Goddess of Love, for example, and a few favoured myths.

Now, after a few years of wandering this path and practicing as a Hellenic pagan, I believe it's incredibly narrow-minded to think of Aphrodite as simply the Goddess of Love, She's rather more complex and the same can be said of all the Theoi, in fact Aphrodite alone has more than 30 different names/titles or Epithets pertaining to her character, appearance, and places she has been worshipped which can be gleaned from reading ancient poems and writings. These are where us Hellenics find our correspondences, especially offerings and ideas for altars. Having a translated copy of the Homeric and Orphic Hymns is incredibly valuable.

I'm also guilty of further narrow-minded statements such as, Hera is the jealous wife of Zeus and Zeus himself is a big flirt. How can you not come to these conclusions based on the myths in those story books or the thousands of association charts out there?

It's OK to come here with those same thoughts, just know that deepening your relationship is about finding all the different facets of a being. I am not only a Hellenic Pagan; I'm also a wife and I work in Mental Health. I am not just one title, and neither are you or our divine beings.

How did I open my mind beyond research and observations? I added another layer of exploration; my own personal experience or UPG (Unverified Personal Gnosis) Now, I've never had a God appear to me to tell me something groundbreaking, other than when I've done guided meditations and I'm not sure that's a God as much as it is my imagination and intuition speaking. I don't hear any whispers from the divine, but I've heard others who have. I believe these people are truly blessed.

If any of this does happen to you, don't be afraid, go with it, you definitely should write about it, make note of the messages - that's a deeply personal experience to do with your relationship with your divine beings. It might be a direction to head, something to look up, an association you hadn't thought of. It's important whatever it is, to you. Sometimes if enough people have had the same experience, and share the same revelation then it might become VPG (Verified Personal Gnosis) or community Gnosis.

I meditate every day. I use a guided meditation app to help me find my breath and the non-judgmental stillness within to observe where I am emotionally and physically. I dedicate this time to Lord Dionysos for taking care of my emotional wellbeing; one of his many facets is to bring and/or cure "madness".

During this time, sometimes I will ask for a message from Lord Apollon or Lord Hermes. Apollon because of his links to the oracle of Delphi and I choose to honour him as Kyklos Apollon on a Sunday (a day of divination in his name) which some Hellenics partake in. Hermes as a messenger God and a being I feel drawn toward in his Psychopompos form (guide of souls) linked very much to working with my shadow and through working in mental health. We'll talk more about dedicating behaviours to the Gods in the next part of this section.

These quiet and sacred spaces may just be the place where messages and hints from these divine beings come through.

In conclusion, other than physical acts of devotion in their many forms, getting to know your God's many facets, titles, associations are incredibly important to the Hellenic Pagan. Not only by reading/researching but by meditating and communing with them.

The Olympians and many more

Not all Hellenics connect with all of the pantheon; I believe you'd be hard pushed to connect with all of the thousands of beings included anyway, remember I've been doing my challenge for a few years now. It's certainly a lifelong commitment! What I do find intriguing is that it seems, like a lot of Pagan paths that the Gods come to us differently.

Although my goal might be to connect with each of the Olympians and the deities associated with them (Persephone is an example of that), some Titans and Primordial deities, the Heroes, spirits, nymphs, creatures etc., that isn't necessarily the goal of every Hellenic Pagan, I've come across, some who worship in much the same way as neo-paganism or Wiccan with a male and female deity, some who work with Titans, some focus on Goddesses, others on Gods specifically The differences are as varied as the Pagan paths themselves, all proudly calling themselves Hellenic Pagans. I would make a point here though in saying that most Hellenic Polytheists will dedicate themselves to the pantheon as a whole.

The Olympians, also known as the Dodekatheon, are the most recognised Gods of Hellas and the most commonly accepted list of Olympians is; Zeus, Hera, Poseidon, Demeter, Athena, Apollo, Artemis, Ares, Aphrodite, Hephaestus, Hermes, and Dionysus.

Most Hellenic Pagans acknowledge that Hestia stepped down from her seat as an Olympian to live amongst us mortals and Dionysus took her place.

I think Hestia is often overlooked and underestimated, so we'll start with Her.

Hestia

A central part of worship in Hellenic Paganism, she is honoured first and last at every ritual, which harkens to her tale of being the first born of Rhea and Kronos, the first swallowed by Kronos and the last disgorged. Those that practice strict Hellenismos will offer Hestia daily morning and evening prayers and sacrifices, believe me when I say that making the time to do this isn't necessary but it is a magical experience and one, I am proud to say I do... most days although I've put my own spin on it. I often say my morning prayer whilst I am engaged in my morning routine, the evening prayer and "sacrifice" of a part of my evening meal happen at the same time. I sometimes offer her hopes for the day ahead in the morning and my troubles and my successes of the day at night.

When she was offered marriage proposals by both Apollon and Poseidon, she refused and asked Zeus to let her remain an eternal virgin. He agreed and she became the eternal flame in the royal hearth of Olympus. She's often depicted veiled or at least modestly dressed. Today, many Hellenic Pagans choose to veil while performing ritual acts and communing with the Theoi in devotional acts. I know of several who choose to veil all the time, I have a lot of respect for these devotees, certainly in the world in which we live now. I only veil if I am in formal ritual at home or working with Chthonic (Underworld) deities because that feels right to me. I have a subtle silver crown of laurel leaves I wear to open rituals with my coven, when I'm able to attend.

She is the sacrificial flame, the fire that cooks the sacrifices for feasting; therefore, she receives a portion of each sacrifice.

She is also, basically, the oven in each home, so presides over the cooking of the family meal, especially bread and receives a portion of that too in thanks for the blessings of the family. Today, many Hellenic Pagan household altars and shrines to Hestia are set up in the kitchen, I've mentioned it before, this is where my space to Hestia is. Like my working altar it includes a candle which is lit while preparing and eating food and an offering plate/libation bowl for the portion of food and drink shared with Her, because a lot of us don't spend all of our time toiling away in the kitchen and we have central heating so don't need a fire going all the time to heat our homes, we have adapted to using electronic candles to symbolise the eternal flame. I have a candle I light when I'm actually cooking that smells of baking cookies and a battery operated one that stays lit all the time.

It's always struck me how little information there is about her, given her importance. She doesn't have a major role in any myth, and yet she is literally the heart or hearth of every home and polis (city state). Her main hearth tended to by her priestesses would have been used to light those in every household. Perhaps that is enough. I like the symbolism of this and choose to keep a light in honour of community, not just of the Hellenist community but the ones I live, work, and play in. It speaks reams that in diving deeper into the history of worship, that Hestia doesn't feature before the creation of the city states, I do wonder if she is part of civilisation, similar to Athena.

I'm trying to show how the modern-day practitioner might bring their practice up to date and make it more relevant to today as I strongly believe part of that task is enquiring whether the divine beings we honour have relevance in our modern world. Hestia is a good example of this; she is family, she is home, she is a safe space, comfort and warmth, she is abundance and plenty. And even if these things are lacking, to me she speaks of protection, charity, being a part of a community and connection to others. These are some of the things that every human being strives to achieve in their journey, think Maslow's Hierarchy of Needs at the very base of human survival and you get Hestia.

Zeus

The almighty Zeus, the King of the Gods and the god of the sky, includes weather, law and order, destiny, fate, and kingship. Forever depicted as a regal, mature man with a sturdy figure and dark beard. Changed by popular culture into a more Abrahamic God figure with a white and/or grey beard.

I've not always connected with Zeus on a mythology level at least; I used to find his frequent philandering rather a turn off, until I meditated on it. I have strong feelings about adultery and cheating which was more than likely not allowing me to connect. What I learned from opening my mind was that the Gods are above moral code, Zeus especially created it, but they didn't have to abide by it.

I tapped into an idea that the Gods were written about in a way that made them more human, something realistic that us mere mortals could relate too. As Xenophanes once wrote. He said "Homer and Hesiod have attributed to the gods all things that bring rebuke and blame among men --- stealing, adultery, deceit." A reminder that mythology would have started with stories around the fire, these stories are not preached at a pulpit on Sundays, they are word of mouth, and let's face it, what's more entertaining than tales of sex and deceit? I can just imagine men gathering at the symposium talking about how Zeus disguised himself as a bull to have sex with Epona.

There's also the theory that the Gods needed heroes, and to make heroes, they had to create them with mortals. Just think, we wouldn't have Herakles without Zeus and his philandering ways. Funny how now my initial thoughts on philandering are turned upside down. I wonder if our modern-day tales of celebrities up to no good will one day become mythologies of our time? And all this from working with Father Zeus! The Gods can help us understand more about the world we live in, the stories of our modern world, the stories we tell ourselves even. For me Zeus helped me explore my moral codes.

Zeus as a sky deity "cloud gatherer", a being presiding over the weather and therefore someone to approach for assisting the earth and avoiding global warming, these aspects could be used in modern times to help with our current environment, although there are, perhaps, more obvious deities out there to work with when referring to the weather. When we look at how Zeus was worshipped in ancient times, we see numerous accounts of how people would sacrifice to Zeus for favourable weather, whether that was about good harvests and the avoidance of famine or the ability to set sail, explore and wage war. Let's not allow that which Zeus is most known for detract from his other aspects.

His fight to free his siblings and forcibly remove the Titans from power is one of his most famous stories. Zeus as the punisher is an interesting aspect, he deals out punishments to those who did wrong and commit acts of impiety. There's a duality to this, he was also seen as Zeus the peacemaker. I see leadership and righting wrongs in the stories that surround both of these sides. Messages of kinship/family, strength and fighting for the little guy. For me, as a mere mortal, Zeus is at least fair minded. At his feet he has the jars of Fate – one full of bad things, another full of good things, he dispenses both with justice (Nike) at his side. Similarly, the time of a mortal's death was carefully weighed in Zeus' golden scales. He is balance, something I believe we all still strive for.

Hera

I asked some friends recently, what comes to mind when I mention the Goddess Hera, almost all of them snickered back at me and said they think of the jealous wife of Zeus. Truly, when you read some of her myths you can see why people would have gotten this impression. Hera took her anger out on the mortal women and their children who got caught up in Zeus' approaches and those that displeased her, but then at least in terms of punishment when displeased, so did most of the Greek deities.

There is evidence to suggest that Hera was worshipped long before her husband (and brother) in places such as Argos, Tiryns and Olympia. She had cults and her first temple at Olympia was dedicated to her before Zeus. Her role as a goddess of marriage and fertility seems to me to be of greater importance to the people than even Zeus' role as king of the gods. When Hera married Zeus, she gained the title Queen of Heavens, which I believe furthers her role as the goddess of "gamos", which means marriage, and seems to include pregnancy, overseeing childbearing and the preparation for adulthood.

Hera was worshipped by females, whose societal responsibilities mostly consisted of getting married and having babies, in fact those that didn't marry were often considered uncivilised, for marriage was civilisation, these women were sent to live in the wilderness and those that married but didn't bare children were considered not quite complete. The latter would be called a "nymphe" and a married mother would be called "gyne" which along with meaning woman also means mother. Patriarchal Greek society believed that you were not a woman unless you were married and a mother. Marriage was the only significant change of status for females; marriage is a rite of passage serving as a transition from childhood to adulthood, not considerate of age or bodily changes. I'm glad this notion has changed over time, in most parts of the world. A window into the very distant past offers an interesting clue as to where our cultural norms may have originated, however.

There have been votive offerings found in Heraion sanctuaries depicting the pomegranate, a fruit that symbolises fertility for agriculture as well as for women; sometimes, therefore, Hera is considered a goddess of agriculture along with many, many,

many other deities!

If Hera was such a co-dependant Goddess on her husband, getting angry and jealous, sitting atop her throne in heaven with her peacock and cuckoo bird, why would there be cults, sanctuaries and countless evidence of worship? I think this suggests she was once a powerful goddess in practice, but eventually her character was reshaped in mythology by the rise of patriarchy, bringing women to heel perhaps!

Although there are diverse views concerning Hera, the one I associate more with is as a protector of marriage, since I am a married woman after all! I worship Hera so she may bless my own union with my husband, and in times of struggle in our relationship I ask for her guidance and blessings There's a part of me that wonders if I've disrespected her when I am facing difficulties in my marriage, but taking responsibility is also something I think the Greeks hold in reverence i.e. it's not always a God's fault, we're human and we do daft things all the time.

I know a midwife who also worships the Old Gods, she told me that midwives in ancient Greece would chant or recite prayers to Hera for a healthy delivery, even though when Hera tried to make a child of her own without the help of Zeus, the result was crippled Hephaestus. It appears that this practice may have calmed and soothed mothers with the image that Hera was protecting and watching over them. This snippet of knowledge helped me revise my thoughts to include Hera as a mother figure and protector. It also got me thinking about patriarchy again, as in according to some stories (written by men) she couldn't make a healthy child without the help of Zeus. Nevertheless, the sacred Gamos celebrated around Valentines' day is probably one of my favourite festivities celebrating the enduring marriage of Zeus and Hera.

Poseidon

When I think of Poseidon I think of a changing temperament (much like the seas he governs) and a somewhat violent mythology. I imagine him with curly flowing hair streaming out behind him and fierce piercing eyes. Easily offended, hot-blooded, and ill tempered, he is also said to be dignified and competitive; for me it's important not to offend him or disagree with his acts.

He is called Earthshaker for a reason, when he strikes the earth with his iconic three-pronged trident, which might have originally been a fish spear, the earth trembles and splits open. When he strikes the sea, waves rise mountain high and winds howl, wrecking ships and drowning those who live on the shores. He is known as the Olympian God of the sea and earthquakes; he is not to be confused with the sea itself – Pontus. He is known for causing major catastrophic events such as floods, and even unleashing his sea monsters in order to get even.

When calm, he stretches out his hand to still the sea and raise new lands out of water. I've often wondered if Poseidon's nature is where we get the association that water is emotional and unpredictable.

I go to the sea when I'm feeling moody, especially when I've had disputes with others. Poseidon had many disputes with both men and gods, most famously for the patronage of Athens with Athena where he offered a gift of a salty stream and she offered the olive tree (guess who won!) and when the hero Odysseus blinded Poseidon's giant cyclops son Polyphemus, Poseidon engaged in a decade long feud sending him off-course on his famous voyage.

An interesting translation of the very old name Poseidon which has come to light in recent times is "husband of earth" or "lord of waters". Plato went as far as to say it means "knower of many things". Nowadays I see Poseidon as a sea god, but "husband of earth" makes me wonder if he may have been a god of the earth and fertility in times forgotten.

He is honoured in the month of Poseidon, which roughly translates to December/January, when the earth would have been seemingly void of crops and the seas are unfavourable for warfare and exploration. It makes sense then that ancient folk unable to go to sea would focus more on the fertility of the land.

Some forget Poseidon is said to be the creator of the horse as well, it's said he was inspired by the foam on high waves, you can see where we might get the idea that the waves when they roll over and crash look like horses when you have the background understanding from these stories.

Just like his brother Zeus, Poseidon had a thing for the ladies, they didn't necessarily return his advances either, therefore, there are many conquests in Poseidon's mythology, most of them unwanted, although he had a faithful wife, the Nereid Amphitrite. His children are many, including the mystical horse Pegasus, the talking horse Arion, and Triton who is half fish, half man, and many mortals. I would suggest looking up Poseidon's family tree on Theoi.com, it's remarkable how fertile this watery being is and adds to the idea that water corresponds to fertility.

I have often debated upon the similarities between the brothers Zeus and Poseidon being two sides of the same coin, an unverified personal gnosis or UPG. As a polytheist I believe them to be separate deities, showing two sides of managing emotions, one of whom shows emotions as raw and natural, untamed if you like and the other attempting to control his emotions and be regal and superior. The power struggle between these two ways of managing emotions has always intrigued me.

I imagine Poseidon with a palace of pearls and shells on the bottom of a beautiful coral reef in the Aegean Sea. I also see him as someone who spends more time on Mt. Olympus because of his jealousy for his brother, despite the incredible fortune of being Lord of the seas. Emotions amplified, just like the sea!

Hades

Although, not widely accepted as an Olympian, I honour Lord Hades. The third of the three brothers who drew lots for dominion over realms, Hades became Lord of the Underworld also named Hades. This is a shadowy place below the earth which is considered the afterlife for the souls of the dead. Hades seldom leaves his realm.

In this modern world, Hades is often romanticised as the bad guy that girls swoon over for his part in the Rape of Persephone. I can see why this is done, the idea of kidnap and imprisonment does not sit well with our modern mind set. Especially when you add in the deception of encouraging her to eat Pomegranate seeds to keep her captive for six months of the year. Many people believe Persephone grew to love Hades and that she becomes a formidable and fearsome queen when she's in the Underworld. Personally, I won't water down the myth, but I will argue that the word "rape" means something completely different now to what it did when it was written. Rape in ancient times seems to have been more akin to kidnap

To the ancients Hades was the most feared of the gods, described by Homer and Hesiod as "pitiless", "loathsome" and "monstrous". There seems to have been a superstitious awe to how Hades was seen by the Greeks. There are some anecdotal accounts of sacrifices happening at night, the blood of the victim left to seep into the earth to reach Hades, thumping the ground three times and when walking away from a chthonic altar, never looking back, and never consuming any part of a sacrifice in chthonic work. The latter superstitions are things I've incorporated into my rituals with Underworld themes. It seems the ancients even feared uttering his name out loud, preferring to use epithets instead. Although Lord of the Underworld, it's worth noting that Hades isn't death, that honour is bestowed upon winged Thanatos.

There was always some controversary with saying "I'm a

devotee of Hades", we simply do not know if he was worshipped with as much reverence as others in ancient times, if he was, I would imagine it would have been done in secret. If I take you back to the term miasma, where we talked about death carrying a lot of it, and the importance of purification before approaching the Gods, you can see why any active worshipping that may have taken place was seen as taboo.

In myth, Hades, apart from being Lord of Hades and the one, along with his three judges, who passes judgement on souls passing through into afterlife, is surprisingly helpful, lending his helmet to aid others; the helmet was made by Hephaistos and rendered the wearer invisible. It helped Athena as she fought with Ares in Homer's account of the Trojan War in the Iliad and Perseus in his quest for the head of Medusa. Perhaps I am somewhat caught in his spell myself...

I have always been interested in the afterlife and the underworld, once considering I might make a good funeral director! Instead I wandered into helping people manage mental health conditions and recover from substance misuse issues. I'm fascinated by shadow work; therefore, I believe I have a very strong connection with the Chthonic realms. I've recently come across a lot of Hellenic Pagans discussing if they work in a way that connects to their Gods. I do, and I'm very proud of that. Not only do I work with the shadows (mental health, recovery, death sometimes) but I also work within health and wellbeing, so I can often be found honouring Apollon and Asklepois (father of medicine).

The wonderful thing about this is, I didn't even realise what I was doing per say, it simply felt right to honour these deities, and to continue to work in this field even when things are tough. As a Hellenic Pagan I don't consider my magical life to be any different to my mundane life, they are my life. It's comforting to see these things in action, deepening that relationship through what might be considered mundane acts continues, even when things change in my work life as they at this current time I see the work of the Gods.

The Underworld

The God Hermes, in his chthonic form psychopompos, is said to lead souls to the river Styx in the underworld, where the aged boatman Charon, for a small fee placed by loved ones in the dead persons mouth during funerary rites, ferries them to the gates of Hades. This is an accepted act, however, as you study you will see it's not universal. As a modern-day Hellenic Pagan, I've discussed this with my husband and I'd like to be cremated, but I'd also like a coin to be buried wherever I am spread.

Anyway, the souls encounter the ferocious three headed dog Kerberos, who stands guard (keeping souls in rather than others out) after the ferry ride. Those having not had the proper send off or who are not given payment for Charon are thought to have been condemned to wander the earth as ghosts. Hades and superstition go hand in hand, but it also eludes to the idea that the underworld cannot be necessarily a place of suffering like the Christian hell. It is simply a place of rest. It also suggests that as a rite of passage, death was incredibly important to the ancient people, there are numerous accounts and a lot of evidence of elaborate funerary rites. Death touched so many so often in the ancient world, it therefore makes sense that a lot was placed on the proper way of honouring loved ones on their next journey. Ancestral worship seems to be another cornerstone of the Hellenic Pagan with practitioners opting to have ancestral altars.

Our souls have navigated the waters of the River Styx and made it to the gates, they are now assessed for their actions whilst alive by three judges. Traditionally these are Minos, Rhadamanthys, and Aiakos. Souls who are judged as having lived a good and pious life drink from the waters of the River Lethe to forget the bad and are given permission to rest in the idyllic Elysian Fields under the rule of Cronus. Those judged to have led a "bad" life would be placed in the hands of the Furies who dish out retribution to those guilty of wrongdoing in Tartarus, the lowest and most tormented level of Hades. Perhaps the Greek understanding of the underworld had nothing to do with the development of heaven and hell at all. Whether the Christian idea of these two realms were somewhat developed from the beliefs of the ancient peoples.

Hades is often depicted with a cornucopia, upon his ebony throne or riding a chariot drawn by black horses. This demonstrates the wealth that comes from the earth not only in plant life and therefore agriculture but in precious metals and stones. Every time I work with crystals or the wealth of the earth, I give thanks to Hades. Although currency is generally considered Hermes' realm, I do believe the metals that make our currency are in Hades' domain.

My actual honouring of Hades consists of prayer, libations and the complete burning of offerings. I tend to work with him in the autumn and winter months. Since there are no festivals in his honour, for obvious reasons, it can be hard to worship him in a reconstructive way.

Artemis

When I first came to Hellenic Paganism, a part of me wanted to be the perfect polytheist. I don't think that's an uncommon goal for people to want to know and do everything "right". For some that looks like creating space for each deity in the pantheon and honouring every single one of them formally and totally. What I am realising is I don't have a connection with all of the Olympians for example but rather with some of them, I am attracted to parts of them, certain epithets or stories.

I don't consider this is a bad thing... and you shouldn't either. It's not ignoring parts; it's respecting those parts but choosing to honour and relate to others.

Take Artemis, for example, very much respected and popular in Hellenic circles, but often referred to as a secondary Goddess. Artemis is the goddess of the hunt, the forest, and hills, she has a moon connection and she loves archery. I respect Artemis as goddess of the wilderness, childbirth and virginity. But it is only the former that really calls to me now. Some years ago, as a younger woman I looked to Artemis for protection - she's a protector of young children specifically girls and young women. I've changed with age and feel I have made it through at least a couple of life changes that no longer put me in the category of child or virgin! I relate more to Hera and Aphrodite now.

Artemis was said to have been born before her brother on the 6th of the month and is therefore honoured every month on the 6th, her twin brother Apollon on the 7th, this might account for her need to protect and nurture. Out of respect I will pour a libation to them on their sacred days and their official annual birthdays, the Thargelia happens around May, which could be associated with Beltane.

Artemis' worship flourished in pre-Hellenic times, there seems to be many cults to her, preserving traces of often localised and lost deities. In Pelopannese in particular, there is some evidence that maidens representing tree nymphs (dryads) would dance to honour her in lavish and wild ways. Throughout Peloponnese, Artemis bears such names as Limnaea and Limatis (Lady of the Lake), this links her in my mind to ancient legends of King Arthur in my own homeland. Wells and springs are important in Celtic custom. Being from the UK, I connect with Artemis specifically on her supervision of wells and springs, waters in lakes and lush wild growth attended to by water nymphs (naiads). I am a nature loving person, I am at home in the wilderness, enjoying long walks through forests and camping as opposed to city life, outdoor pursuits and being a member of some nature charities, such as the RSPB, are ways in which I honour Artemis rather than ritual and sacrifice.

The Nymphs

They are essentially nature spirits, usually female, nurturing, often lovers and sometimes motherly beings. Not quite Goddesses although long lived and beautiful. I have a very strong connection with them, I have a list of some of the nymphs I've become accustomed to making offerings too when I am in their domain. This is not an exhaustive list, I encourage you to find out more about them, and I also encourage you to go to the natural areas you live in and try to connect with them in meditation and by making animal and environmentally friendly offerings. They are as follows: Alseids – Groves, Dryads – Forests, Hydriads – Water, Leimoniads – Meadows, Naiads – Springs and rivers, Napaea – Valleys, Nereid – the Mediterranean Sea, Oceanids – the sea, and, Oreads – mountains

An example I have of my own experience with nymphs is visiting a local pond/lake in a local forest to us. It is genuinely a beautiful almost liminal space, even though it's man-made, it has a wonderful energy. We often take some food for the birds and some vegetables for the donkeys. I will often make a libation of fresh filtered water to the nymphs and hum a sweet song as we walk. I've also discovered through meditation that they like sweet things. I don't, leave a cake or sweets for them because of the impact that might have on the natural environment, however, I have been known to have a picnic including cake, left out long enough for the nymphs to take their fill and then the crumbs are disposed of in a sensitive and appropriate way before we leave.

Apollon

Apollon is another example of a deity I only relate to on certain platforms, although he's popular, important in Hellenic circles and complex. God of many things, he presides over art, the sun, light, knowledge, poetry, music, and medicine to name but a few. Apollon is seen as an ideal male – youthful and athletic in form. Like his sister he protects youngsters, particularly young males and like his sister can bring about death and disease, sometimes in the form of pests in agriculture, the festival of Thargelia is celebrated as a means of seeking a blessing from Apollon and Artemis (the Shining twins) to protect the main harvest of the year from pests and disease.

For many musicians and poets, Apollon is God of the arts, for others he is a light or sun God and sometimes depicted with the same halo of light that surrounds depictions of Jesus in art. Personally I connect with the Titan Helios as the sun, as much as I see the Titan Selene as the moon rather than Artemis. This is a good example of how OK it is to see other deities as more prominent over certain areas than others. I tend to walk the line between the Golden Age and Classical periods, often opting for Titans for personifications of certain things in nature.

I connect with Apollon on two levels, as an Oracular God, patron of the centre of the ancient spiritual world - Delphi and as a God of music and poetry. When I use my oracle cards, pendulum, coins or knuckle bones to divine I am honouring Apollon and Hermes. Apollon for the gifts of prophecy and Hermes for delivering the message.

Delphi is an ancient site, believed to have been a domain of the earth mother Gaia before Apollon came down from Olympus and defeated a great snake who guarded a sacred cave making the site a centre of prophecy, and using the Oracle Pythia to deliver messages from the Gods to the people. Thousands of people are said to have made pilgrimages to Delphi to receive predictions for the future, in fact as a spiritual hub, it might just rival the seat of the Eleusinian Mysteries, Elysium or the Parthenon in Athens.

Demeter

We've looked at the three brothers and their sisters, Hera and Hestia. The other sister to mention is Demeter. The Goddess Demeter is a reincarnation of local mother-Earth goddesses who would have been worshipped in rural communities. Despite her being, according to popular myth, one of Zeus' sisters she appears to be much older than that.

Writers of old searched long and hard to explain the turning of the seasons, they believed the Horai or Horae (hours) were the goddesses of the seasons and the order of nature would turn the wheel so to speak. The origins story for the seasons you might be more familiar with comes from the tale of the maiden Kore (Persephone) and her mother Demeter. This tale to be incredibly important to my own practice, more so than any other tale it is the one that led me down this path.

The story tells us that the beautiful maiden Kore (daughter of Demeter) was out picking flowers in meadows with her nymph friends, when a daffodil created by Zeus to tempt her, caught her attention, when she picked it, the earth opened up and she was kidnapped by Hades and taken into his realm to be his queen. The common thought is this took place in a neighbourhood of Eleusis, and therefore Eleusis became Demeter's seat of worship and power and there is born one of the most famous mystery cults. Demeter goddess of harvest and the fertility of the earth was distraught and started to neglect her role to earths fertility, she wandered the earth for nine days in search of her daughter without nectar or ambrosia and without bathing. I think of her as Goddess of the natural cycle of life and death.

She came across Hekate who had heard the maiden's cries and with her shining torches they continued the search. She learned that Zeus had promised Hades he could have Kore as his consort from Helios. So angry was Demeter that she refused to return to Olympus. She severely punished any mortal who did not receive her gifts with proper reverence or those who repulsed her. She eventually produced a famine on the Earth, stopping growth altogether.

Zeus feared the race of mortals would become extinct, so he sent all the gods of Olympus to appease her with presents.

Negotiations opened eventually, and Zeus sent Hermes to Hades to retrieve Kore (now married and known as Persephone). Hades consented but gave Persephone part of a pomegranate to eat, in order to tie her to his realm. Hermes Psychopomp delivered Persephone back to her mother in Eleusis on Hades' chariot. Hekate became, and remains to this day, an attendant and companion of Persephone. Zeus granted that Persephone would spend part of the year in subterranean darkness, and part of it with her mother.

When Kore descends into Hades her mother Demeter mourns (Autumn) and eventually stops earth's growth (Winter), when Persephone ascends back to the earth her mother rejoices and the earth grows again (Spring) she is so happy the world flourishes (Summer).

The most wonderful part of the worship of Demeter are the Eleusinian Mysteries, the most famed of the mysterious rites and cults, in later years Homer's great Hymn to Demeter was written revolving around the symbolic representation of the story of Demeter and Persephone, symbolising life, death and even immortality, which also gives us a template for what the Mysteries might have involved. An accepted thought is that the Mysteries themselves give initiates confidence to face death and a promise of bliss in Hades. Today all we have are broken pieces of information, creating controversy amongst historians who try to puzzle together this ancient tradition.

The Mysteries

My path concentrates around the Eleusinian. I do encourage you to research as best you can other mystery cults, as what we do know is fascinating and engaging, often making up a large part of the Hellenic Pagan path. The other is the Orphic tradition.

Modern scholars believe that the rituals involved in worshipping the goddess Demeter existed before stories were composed to explain them. And these stories in the form of songs were gradually incorporated into the rituals which honour them.

There is a major moral point in the Homeric Hymn to Demeter concerning hospitality - being kind and welcoming to strangers as they may be gods in disguise, walking among us, and another is related to how even Zeus isn't above the laws of nature.

The truly epic hymn reminds us that the rituals of Demeter are sacred and celebrate the rebirth of grains after they have been underground. This impresses upon the reader the great powers and mysteries of the Goddess.

To me the same regenerative forces that end up replenishing the earth and heralding bounty are also the same thing that bring about coldness and a sense of desolation to the earth. Demeter must live with the joy of being with her daughter Persephone but is also abound to live with her absence. She is incapable of living a life that is totally present with happiness. By the same token she is relieved of living a life of total despair. A sense that as beings, this too shall pass, that we are able to bridge both experiences that bring us happiness and ones that bring us hurt.

The journey of transformation that the maiden Kore experiences is more of a modern concept, in the hymn itself Kore/ Persephone is barely mentioned. Our modern sense of female empowerment has moved modern worship to celebrate how Kore faced her circumstances and became Persephone, Queen of the Underworld. In my path I also acknowledge that Hades isn't so much the philander his brothers are, for the most part he is faithful to his queen. You can see where a great love story and power couple has emerged and perhaps that is why the story itself resonates so much to a modern Hellenic Pagan.

It's worth remembering that the mysteries themselves centre around Demeter. Details of the rites and celebrations which took place during all mystery initiations and subsequent membership were sworn under oath by initiates and therefore have vanished from our knowledge. The penalty for breaking this oath – death! However, we have fragments of accounts of initiates especially around the Eleusinian. Some things historians tend to agree on are that whilst Demeter was in Eleusis, she ordered a temple and altar be built in her honour, this is called the Telesterion, a sort of underground theatre where the sacred and secret part of the rites took place. Anyway, after the reunion with her daughter she instructed the leaders of Eleusis in how to perform her rites. The cult, then, is believed to have been taught directly by Demeter.

There are different levels of initiation to the cult and three categories of events – Dromena (things which were enacted), Deiknumena (things which were shown) and Logomena (things which were explained). The mysteries are broken down into two parts with other festivals throughout the year that can be related to them. The main two parts are the Lesser mysteries that are celebrated in spring, this week long festival relates to purification in preparation for the Greater Mysteries in Autumn. For those of you looking to use the modern Celtic Wheel of the Year as a point of reference, the Greater Mysteries would be around Mabon and the Lesser Mysteries around Ostara – the Equinoxes, as times of the balance between light and dark, death and rebirth.

What I will do every year is make it a priority to celebrate at the very least the festivals that are thought to be related to the mysteries.

A central part of the Eleusinian rites seems to have involved drinking Kykeon. It's thought to have been a barley and mint beverage, although it's been suggested it might have also had some sort of hallucinogenic effect which would produce a psychedelic experience. Then the initiates would enter the Telesterion, symbolic of the death and rebirth of Persephone being underground and which may have involved some sort of reference to altered states of consciousness. As a modern-day Hellenic who will admit to being largely sober, I do not advocate the use of substances, I find my altered states of consciousness through meditation, drumming and dancing.

According to many, people flocked to Eleusis and other centres of mystery cults in antiquity for a chance to be initiated into the mysteries from all over the civilised world, men, women, and children, (free men or women unstained by crime), even slaves. Not only rural peasants but leaders as well. I think this air of inclusivity is what also draws me to worship in this way. It was the emperor Theodosius who issued edicts against mystery cults in the late fourth century CE. Up until that point the Eleusinian Mysteries quickly assumed the status of the most important and widely attended mystery cult in the Greek-speaking world.

Historians do know that those who participated in the mysteries were forever changed for the better and that they no longer feared death. The initiates returned from their pilgrimage to Eleusis full of joy and happiness, and filled with hope of a better life in the world of shadows.

Mystery cults existed at the same time as regular religious practice, such as household practice and city state festivities. Individuals made a personal decision to enter a mystery cult through initiation, using them as a supplement to the common religion.

Another popular set of Mysteries in Hellenic Paganism is the Dionysian or Bacchic Mysteries, dedicated to the God Dionysos/Dionysus and/or Bacchus. He is the god of wine and vegetation and these mysteries often used intoxicants and trance inducing activities to remove inhibitions and remove civilised societal norms. These mysteries seem to have brought the participants to a primordial nature, and offered a sense of liberation to those marginalised in normal society like women, slaves, outlaws and non-citizens.

The Bacchic mysteries began in the late archaic period, if not before. It's thought around 600 BCE in Corinth, based on vase paintings depicting Bacchic revelry. The Dithyrambos, a cult hymn seems to have been invented in Corinth and the ruling clan of Corinth called Bacchaidai claimed descent from Dionysos.

The mysteries were spread by wandering clergy throughout Greece, they were of both genders, claiming knowledge of the mysteries which stretched back to teachings directly from Dionysos, although it seems by 210 BCE in Hellenistic Egypt Ptolemy IV Philopater required any clergy performing initiations register in Alexandria and list three generations of teachers. Proving your legitimacy seems to stretch back into the very distant past... I don't believe as a Hellenic Pagan you need to prove anything, one of the things I genuinely loathe is folk claiming knowledge over others, having access to some ancient wisdom and then narrow mindedly shutting others out because they are not descendent. No one has the right to make you feel inadequate in your journey.

What we do know is Bacchic initiation has four stages, conceiving the desire to join and apply, preparation, sacred rites and the final stage in integration with other initiates. Artwork and some texts seem to show both women and man were initiated and that it wasn't confined to the Greek population. There seems to have been two attractions for people to join the mysteries, a renewal after a release from madness and similar to the Eleusinian a promise of a good afterlife.

After the sixth century BCE, there began a crossover between the two mysteries offering a blissful afterlife as opposed to reincarnation or an unconscious memory void existence in Hades. They crossed over in a number of ways, by associating Iacchos (he who leads the Eleusinian's great procession from Athens to Eleusis) with Dionysos. Based on the similarity of their names, the nature of the great procession being frenzied with dancing, laughter, singing and some thought intoxication and also the festival Lenaia were Iacchos was called the son of Semele (mother of Dionysos in earlier myth). Connecting Dionysos with his Chthonic nature and the mysteries is also thought to be achieved by wearing garlands of white poplar (associated with the underworld) during Dionysos/Bacchic rites.

Dionysos

Just like Demeter, Dionysos has his beginnings in pre-Greek culture, Mycenaean Linear B script used from about 1500-1100 BCE shows worship of Dionysos at Pylos and a temple built in the Minoan period which was in continuous use throughout the Greek period had an inscription marking it as a sanctuary that belongs to Dionysos. His worship spans into the Roman period where he became Bacchus.

Dionysos, to me, is ancient. Contrary to myths, in Hesiod's Theogony for example, where the mortal Semele gives birth to him following an intimate encounter with Zeus, where she then becomes a goddess. Later mythology says Semele couldn't stand Zeus' affection and dies as a result. Zeus rescues the fetus and carries it to term in his thigh.

The version which interests me personally is the one common to the Dionysian or Bacchic Mysteries where Dionysus was born of Goddess Persephone with Zeus as his father. This version has Dionysos sat upon the throne in the Underworld and then enticed by Titans, who murder him and tear him to pieces before being born again. This is another reminder that Myths are stories, and stories change, having little to nothing to do with actual religious worship in Ancient times, because there are numerous versions from differing writers and areas.

Dionysos is often associated with madness and frenzy that descends upon his worshippers, he is also considered a god who can cure madness. The mysteries are said to cure suffering and afflictions of the mind, allowing people to express their emotions in a frenzy which was considered to a divine revelation, even possession by Dionysos himself. I've noticed like-minded individuals in the pagan community who also work within mental health have Dionysos as a main deity to honour.

I love the idea that Dionysos seems to have brought people across the Med together throughout different periods in history. He has an inclusive nature and he is often associated with the LGBT+ communities. Dionysos is a complex God and it's worth exploring his many facets. One the most frustrating generalisations I see is Dionysos is all about parties and getting drunk... yes, he brought wine making to mankind and his celebrations are often both sombre and celebratory. But he is often misunderstood and I encourage you to challenge those thoughts going forward.

Hermes

Myths such as his involvement in escorting Pandora, Perseus and Priam are worth a read for his roles as a herald. He carries the famous kerykeion (the herald's staff) and is often depicted wearing winged sandals for the swiftness of his messages.

Such myths as releasing Io from the many eyed monster Argos and Ares from twin giants Otus and Ephialtes are worth dipping into to see why for me he is "the darling of the gods" especially to his father Zeus.

Hermes has a cheeky kind of energy woven into his deeply divine, and, maddening nature, if you're looking for mischief, Hermes is your god. He is the god of many things similar to his half-brother Apollon, including trade, wealth, luck, fertility, animal husbandry, sleep, language, thieves, and travel.

Hermes is forever connected to the wilderness as well as pastoral regions with origins, some historians say, as an Arcadian fertility god. Because of his association with the land and trade Hermes is also associated with travelers and most likely strangers, historically travelers held Hermes as their patron, piles of rocks known as herm or herma with a phallus symbol and/or head (usually depicting Hermes) were often set up along road sides, marking a trail, milestones or a boundary in some cases, these are also known as cairns, you see them even now on country roads around England. I have a small pile of rocks by my front door as I live in an apartment, which marks my boundary! Ancient Greeks likely marked the front of their homes in a similar fashion.

There's a link here with Hekate, people would leave offerings often at crossroads, also where hermae could be found and where travelers would partake in these offerings. The offerings were often left at Hekate's' Deipnon (dark of the moon) an auspicious time we've discussed previously. This connection to strangers and feeding people who wander has led to a modern-day practice where some will make an offering to food banks and charities that support the homeless.

Hermes has something similar to an impish character, with a need to fulfil his amusement. Whilst still a baby, Hermes is said to have stolen Apollon's sacred herd of cattle, and reversed the imprint of their hooves to make them harder to track, hence his association with thieves. In the end he kept the cattle and created the lyre, a stringed instrument similar to a harp for Apollon. As a trickster Hermes is known to have stolen Artemis' arrows, Aphrodite's girdle and Poseidon's trident.

He is often associated with gambling, luck and wealth, for his creation of dice, which are the tip of the iceberg in terms of creations – fire, musical instruments, the alphabet are also included in this list. The language part is interesting, he seems to have been credited with excellent communication and diplomacy skills; when I'm facing conflicts, communication difficulties, or in need of writing inspiration, I will pray to Hermes.

Ares

Moving through the family tree of males, we arrive at Ares another son of Zeus and Hera. Ares features seldomly in my worship, he is more of a lesson for me (I'm an Aries). When you look at the Attic calendar you realise Ares doesn't feature very often in celebrations. When you read a little more about him, you might understand why. Ares is often described as a blood-lust God of battlefields whose famous myths include having an adulterous affair with the Goddess Aphrodite, and turning into a boar to gorge Aphrodite's love Adonis out of jealousy.

Of course, there are other sides to Ares, that of civil order for example and dishing out justice for events like his daughter being raped. This is my personal connection to him and chances are it will not match that of every Hellenic Pagan. So, for me, he is lust and he is the frenzied bloody battlefield, as opposed to the strategy and logic in war Athena provides. A lot of Ares worship comes from the battlefield, where soldiers would pray to him for a successful battle and the courage to carry out bloody endeavors under the orders of their commanders.

Ares battle myths are also often accompanied by how he was wounded and would flee back to Olympus bellowing in pain or how he got himself trapped in a bronze jar for example whilst defending Olympus. I think the morals of these myths are around blindly entering battle and how acting on pure raw emotion and split-second decisions will often result in harm to self and others.

This quote from the Homeric Hymn to Ares sums up how I personally choose to work with the raw energy of Ares –

"...Shed down a kindly ray from above upon my life, and strength of war, that I may be able to drive away bitter cowardice from my head and crush down the deceitful impulses of my soul. Restrain also the keen fury of my heart which provokes me to tread the ways of blood-curdling strife. Rather, O blessed one, give you me boldness to abide within the harmless laws of peace, avoiding strife and hatred and the violent fiends of death." (Homeric Hymn to Ares, Translated by H. G. Evelyn-White, 1914)

I choose to use his message to be mindful of my actions.

Heroes

One of the most popular areas of worship to many Hellenic

Pagans is Hero worship... another diversion on our journey through the Olympians...

This takes into account the stories of mortals who have endured great trials and tribulations to become some of the most celebrated characters in myth and legend. They feature hugely in popular culture and paved the way for the superhero movement. Throughout time we have needed heroes to remind us that our struggles can be turned into great strength, to offer reason to why we go through what we go through and to have faith that it'll probably turn out OK in the end. The deeper meaning of the hero has a lot of empowerment.

The Greeks also needed a good story, one where they felt closer to the Divine in the same way we do. Like the Daimones who bridge the gap between mankind and the divine, the heroes do too. This relates strongly to honouring ancestors, we all have heroes in our histories in one way or another. It's evidenced in the elaborate funerary rites we've touched upon that ancestor worship was significant in ancient times and the fact that we still talk and honour heroes today either personally, or in a wider context like our troops engaged in combat, makes me think this kind of worship is why Hellenic Paganism is gaining such popularity.

We honour the heroes in festivals, there are some dedicated to some more popular heroes like Herakles for example; equally if you dive into other polias calendars you will find festivities dedicated to local heroes in ancient times. They are often about prayer and offering libations, and are not necessarily elaborate.

By looking up the history of your region you can discover heroes from your own land to honour and you can explore your own family tree you can look for people who you can honour in your own ways. We do this simply, in story-telling, for example, in acts of courage and overcoming our own personal trials and tribulations, and, by understanding what went before.

My personal worship of heroes does include honouring

Greek heroes, but more in terms of reading the stories and understanding the lessons, I will pour a libation around the Attic celebrations of heroes, but I'm unlikely to elaborate. In a more practical sense, my personal worship has included setting up an ancestor altar, exploring my family tree, going to France to visit the battlefields of WW1 and WW2 and wearing a poppy in November. Simple acts. Simple nods to heroes in my own family and those of my land. Even though I do not condone war, these events happened in our histories and for me I feel that honouring the journeys of people in the past is hugely humbling for me in the present as I face my own journey.

Hephaistos

Also spelt Hephaestus, the lame son of Hera. Born with a clubbed foot. The myth I favour was that Hera was humiliated by him and threw him from Olympus where he was raised by two sea nymphs and learned the gift of craftmanship.

I quite like Hephaistos, to me he symbolises a person who doesn't fit, portrayed as a burly, muscular man, with a thick neck and hairy chest, his clubfoot caused him to limp or at least walk with a rolling gait. He was a target for the mockery of the "perfect" Olympians, he was unsure of his parentage and unlucky in love. His myths tell of adultery and rejection. But I consider Hephaistos a genius, because even though all of that labelled him, he was the only God who actually worked, and therefore he has a large following in those people who are creative. I believe he channeled much of his sense of rejection and anger into his craft as God of blacksmiths, stonemasonry, craftmanship and the God of Fire.

He built his workshop in a volcano deep in the earth, he made palaces for the Olympians, is said to have made Zeus' thunderbolts and scepter, Apollon's golden chariot, his arrows and Artemis' as well, a sickle for Demeter, weapons for Athena, armor for Achilles, Hades Helm and many more beautiful things described in the myths.

He is earthy, with passionate feelings and instincts to rival even the most intuitive. He liked both men and women and used his body. When he tried to interact with the Olympians, they treated him cruelly, even when they saw his wife Aphrodite's infidelity, but when Hephaistos was at work in his forge, his skillful use of fire made him a master of transformation.

Hephaistos speaks to people who feel deeply, where expressiveness and beauty is buried inside and might not be able to be articulated as such, but comes out in creative aspects of the self. The fire of the forge being the unexpressed passion that inspires creativity. His work as a means to heal the wounds of his deformity and rejection. The promise of Hephaistos, to me, is that it is possible to overcome adversity, handicap and any humiliation, and to become respected for works of beauty and precision. When I am creating, especially writing where it's a lonely passionate endeavor for me, I will offer my thoughts and prayers to Hephaistos. When I am planning or strategising, I will combine his energy with that of Athena.

Aphrodite

Aphrodite is perhaps one of the most widely worshipped of the Olympians, she is very popular in Hellenic and on general pagan/goddess worship paths. She is the Goddess of love, beauty, pleasure, and, procreation. The most beautiful of all the goddesses in terms of appearance. Her birth from the castration of Uranus and sea foam is one of the most popular versions from the Theogony and has led to some of the most famous art works over time.

Aphrodite turns up in a lot of myth, she seems to turn up and cause absolute chaos! Tales of mortals and deities falling in love, including her love for the mortal Adonis, whereby she warned him of his hunting pursuits, but he ignored her and was killed by a boar, he was granted permission to return to her for part of the year, similar to the tales of Persephone and Demeter whereby Persephone returned so the love felt by her mother would rejuvenate the earth after the long winter months, Adonis' return is about true love always finding a way.

Conception of new life is a realm of Aphrodite, including Harmony when two passionate energies come together in Ares and Aphrodite, don't forget that equally their union created Phobos (fear) and Deimos (terror), or Hermaphroditus who represents bisexuality and androgyny when Aphrodite united with Hermes.

Zeus tried to stop her amorous ways by marrying her to Hephaistos, but a little thing like marriage was never going to stop Aphrodite, who on the one hand signifies independence, an energy never victimised or made to suffer by men, a being who does what she wants, when she wants, and lives to satisfy her own pleasures, but who is also described as weak and frightened, as well ill-tempered and easily offended.

Aphrodite is confusing, she also has a protective mother side, which is best described in the tale of Psyche and Eros, where her son Eros falls in love with the beautiful Psyche who has been elevated by locals for her beauty. Aphrodite becomes jealous, imprisons Eros and puts Psyche through ruthless trials to prove her love.

So sometimes she's benevolent and kind, sometimes she's fickle and cruel, which to me isn't surprising, she's a divine interpretation of something potentially amazing and thoroughly miserable... love. The interesting part is that philosophers couldn't quite get this divide in her personality, so they split Aphrodite, the benevolent and kind part became Aphrodite Urania who was depicted as divine love, the rest went to Aphrodite Pandemos, the people's Aphrodite.

It was pretty rare for a God to be honoured by everybody. Unless you were a blacksmith, for example, you probably wouldn't worship Hephaistos. Aphrodite on the other hand seems to have been relevant to almost everybody, Zeus as God of the Hellenic world is the other exception. It makes sense, there aren't many people where love, sex, and beauty aren't relevant.

Part 4 – Magic and Mysticism

Let's look at this from the Hellenismos point of view first. According to many followers of this religion, magic does not feature in their practice. To me, I don't think you need magic to walk this path and it's more a matter of understanding and choice. Magic to some is about using power within yourself, your will and intent if you like to make a change, therefore also bending the divine/Universe to your needs, which in terms of Hellenismos ethics would fall firmly into the category of Hubris. This makes magic a controversial subject in Hellenic circles.

I've thought about what magic means to me, it's a good idea for you to explore this as well. It's complicated, because whilst a deer in the forest stopping a little longer and staring at me whilst I was contemplating a decision to me is absolutely a message from Artemis and is indeed a magical experience, I do not see it as magic, but an example of the relationships I am cultivating with the Divine. In the ancient mind frame, they probably would have seen that experience as the Goddess Artemis appearing to me.

I don't think the ancients discounted magic, they had a Goddess of Witchcraft after all in Hekate, who through literature alone went from being a Goddess of wealth, prosperity and kindness to being the old hag associated with the moon, witchcraft, crossroads, necromancy and restless spirits, as the rise of patriarchy occurred.

By 700BC, when Homer wrote the Odyssey, it had already become frowned upon and moved from being a herbal healing type practice to... well, Circe, a female who was feared by all accounts for her ability to poison and turn men into pigs, and then we have the many representations of Medea in tragedy, mythology, and poetry - the stereotypical dangerous woman who engaged in the art of pharmakon or sorcery and magic to frighten people.

The term "witch" seems to have been what was cast upon an older woman who was obsessed with erotic magic, who had the gods under their command, could control the elements, converse with the dead, and strike a victim dumbstruck with one look of their evil eye.

Most Hellenics, me included, do not see things like consulting an oracle, divination, or casting lots to predict the future as magic. In fact, we've talked about one oracle already – Pythia, of Delphi. People would come from miles around to visit the oracle to receive a divine message. The Prophetic seer was incredibly important in ancient times.

Another example of non-magic on the Hellenic path, which might be categorised as magic in a modern sense is the use of sheep knuckle bones known as Astragali which would be cast and read for messages from the divine something akin to the Runes.

The Hellenic path is more about the path of a Mystic if you're going to practice anything that might be considered "magical". Admittedly there is a lot of skepticism within the community especially with regard to seers, as to whether that is actually possible. And because there are little to no accounts of how the altered states of consciousness were achieved in ancient times without the use of intoxication that is a mystery.

As someone who does work with divination, oracle cards and my own version of Astragali, I've pulled on research into Shamanism and the Chinese I-Ching, for example, to help me. I can't say I'll ever be able to put the "tools" down and let go enough to receive direct communication from the Gods. I meditate a lot, but I'm also aware a lot of what I experience within those meditations is my own inner workings rather than the divine, though I still believe it's possible with training and hard work.

What I find really interesting is the practice of Necromancy, or invoking the spirits of the dead. It was considered a form of illegal ritual, but evidence suggests that it was practiced. The spirits of the dead are thought to have possessed abilities that the living did not have, including the power to foretell the future, we've already discovered that the Greeks had elaborate funerary rites and some took part in mysteries regarding life, death, and rebirth.

There is evidence that temples were built in places thought to be entrances to the realm of Hades where necromancy was practiced to receive prophecies. The Necromanteoin dedicated to Hades and Persephone was one of these places.

So, whilst most flocked to Delphi or the like for their prophecy, some did practice this "darker" art form. As it was illegal, we don't really have records of how this was practiced.

There seems to have been a very fine line between magic, superstition, religion and science. Spells and incantations had been used by the Egyptians for thousands of years. As evidenced by the surviving Greek papyri containing magic records that date back to around the 4th and 3rd centuries, the Greeks continued some of these practices, albeit maybe in secret. These instructions for "spells" are fascinating to read, they cover things like how to get over illness, get rid of vermin, make your own amulet, attract a lover, improve your sex life, and include recipes for poisons using rare herbs and exotic spices and incenses.

Practitioners of magic (mageia) the first known to the Greeks were thought to be priests of Persia. They were seen as wise holders of secrets, masters of mathematics and chemistry, but also feared for their associations with death and evil doing. Their lives would have existed on the fringes of society, but people would have sought them out to help them with their daily lives, to overcome struggles and find happiness. Their art included such practices as spells and evil prayers (epoidai), curse tablets (katadesmoi), enhancing drugs and deadly poisons (pharmaka), amulets (periapta) and love potions (philtra).

By the 5th century the penalty for a man and his family found guilty of harmful magic was death, meaning the ancients did believe. The sheer amount of evidence found in archaeological digs suggests if you wish there to be, that there is a place for magic for some.

Periapts, which seem to have been divided into two categories, talismans which were thought to bring good luck and, say, cure a physical ailment or win in a competition, and phylacteries which covered protection like warding off evil, keeping robbers away and protecting you from bad magic, were thought to have been worn around the neck or wrist, or even placed in the home to provide intended results, desires and positive outcomes for situations. Is this magic or superstition? Farmers were thought to be most susceptible to this practice, hoping for favourable weather.

The materials used for talismans included bones, wood, rocks and sometimes gemstones, with bloodstone being the most common. There were sometimes written incantations on small pieces of papyrus or on metal sheets that were carried in small pouches sometimes mixed with herbs. To complete the incantation or spell, a god or goddess needed to be invoked and words of power were spoken out loud.

I love to make amulets out of whatever I come across, especially what is now known as spell bags. I often imbue a semi-precious stone with my intent and carry it with me, and have been known to make symbols out of clay to place around my home.

Many sheets of metal have been found, usually lead, which have been rolled or folded, sometimes nailed shut, fragments of papyrus, limestone, even pottery inscribed with curses. These are the katadesmoi (curses tablets), done to cause harm to enemies. Another form was a clay or wax figurine made to look like a victim but twisted, stuck with nails, and often bound and buried in a miniature lead coffin, sounds a lot like a voodoo doll.

These were like types of hexes done in absolute secrecy, often buried with the dead, because they were believed to have the means to carry the curse requests to Hades. Curse tablets often began with "I bind to the earth…" and have been found in wells as well as simply buried away from dwellings.

I'm not one to advocate curses and hexes, although I don't subscribe to anything like the threefold law or the Wiccan Rede, I don't believe in harming. I see bindings and the occasional banishing as forms of protection and releasing/letting go. I tend to work with the moon phases and use modern day correspondences to pick my herbs and crystals.

The magic I dip my toes in has to be absolutely necessary, I have to be 100% sure that there are no other ways of manifesting what I desire in the mundane or through prayer and communing with the Gods. Although the act of honouring the Theoi to me has never been about what they can do for me.

I've found the more I wander this path, the more I want to be open to the blessings of the Theoi, their teachings and guidance as opposed to manifesting anything in particular, even the thought of bending any beings will feels wrong and with that trust and openness I've found I have been blessed. Sometimes in ways I don't understand to begin with!

I've made myself aware of some of the other forms of magic practiced in ancient times because it fascinates me. I created an effigy of a person I was experiencing problems with once, and did a banishing/binding using my interpretation of what I've described above, the outcome was effective, the person was removed from my life, however the way in which it was done whether circumstantial or not scared me. Be careful what you wish for, as they say.

Closing thoughts from a Modern Hellenic Pagan

Everything done on this path should be done with respect and reverence for all things, whether that is mother nature herself, your fellow human being or the divine.

I believe, in a sympathetic nod toward the past, that although we will never recreate the past, we can use historical evidence to explore the ways in which people interacted with the world around them; their thoughts on how the divine work is just as relevant today as it was then.

Hellenic Paganism is a living path, you literally walk it every single minute of the day, from elaborate rituals and offering, to praying and asking for guidance, to the occasional amulet for protection and good luck. It helps us make sense of this world and combined with modern-day discoveries in science and medicine, it enhances our lives.

It's not separate from the mundane. A meal shared with family, is a sacred meal, the work we choose to do is often linked to our love of the Gods, our passions and hobbies, or where we choose to spend our time often have a relation to the path we walk.

The Hellenic Path is a set of values and ethics, a way to live a good life and strive to be the best possible versions of ourselves. It's rich in historical evidence and varies across individuals, groups, countries and continents. It's welcoming and understanding, intelligent and intuitive. It's adaptable and once you've nailed the most confusing parts it's actually quite easy to see the divine in everything.

For those of you who have picked up this book because you're interested in beginning a Hellenic path, good luck as you start your journey. I hope I've helped you along your way.

For those of you just curious about other paths to your own, welcome to Hellenic Paganism, I hope the work here as given you some insight and ideas of how you might wander your own path.

For those already honouring the great Greek Pantheon and on a Hellenic path, I hope I have done what I can to broadly explore the basics of being a Hellenic Pagan. May the Theoi forever bless you.

Further Reading and Resources

Books

Aldridge, Chris, Hellenic Polytheism: A Personal Guide for Ancient Greek Practitioners (Lulu.com 2017)

Alexander, Timothy Jay, A Beginners Guide to Hellenismos (Lulu Press, Inc 2007)

Alexander, Timothy Jay, Hellenismos Today (Lulu Press, Inc 1782)

Apollodorus, The Library of Greek Mythology (Oxford World's Classics) (Trans) Robin Hard, (OUP Oxford, 2008)

Broad, William J., The Oracle: The Lost Secrets and Hidden Message of Ancient Delphi, (New York: Penguin Press, 2006)

Burkert, Walter, Ancient Mystery Cults, (Cambridge: Harvard University Press, 1987)

Burkert, Walter, Greek Religion (Cambridge: Harvard University Press, 1985)

Burkert, Walter, Sacrificial Ritual and Myth, (Trans Peter Bing), (Berkley: University of California Press, 1983)

Campbell, Drew, Old Stones. New Temples. (Xlibris, 2000)

Collins, Derek, Magic in the Ancient Greek World (Blackwell Ancient Religions) (Wiley-Blackwell, 2011)

Connelly, Joan Breton, Portrait of a Priestess: Women and ritual in Ancient Greece. (Princeton, NJ: Princeton University Press, 2007)

Cosmopoulos, Michael B., ed. Greek Mysteries: The Archaeology and Ritual of Ancient Greek Secret Cults. (London: Routledge, 2003)

Detienne, Marcel and Giulia Sissa, The Daily life of the Greek Gods, (Trans Janet Lloyd, Stanford, Calif: Stanford University Press, 2000)

Evelyn-White, Hugh G., trans Hesiod, Homeric Hymns, Epic Cycle and Homerica. (Cambridge: Harvard University Press, 1936)

Faraone, Christopher J, ed, Initiation in Ancient Greek Rituals and

Narratives. (New York: Routledge, 2003)

Festugiere, Andre-Jean, *Personal Religion Among the Greeks*, (University of California Press, 1960)

Fry, Stephen. *Mythos: The Greek Myths Retold: A Retelling of the Myths of Ancient Greece,* (London, Penguin 2018)

Fry, Stephen. *Heroes: Mortals and Monsters, Quests and Adventures,* (London, Michael Joseph, 2018)

Garland, Robert, *The Greek Way of Life: From Conception to Old Age.* (Ithaca, NY: Cornell University Press, 1992)

Garland, Robert, *The Greek Way of Death.* (Ithaca, NY: Cornell University Press, 2001)

Graf, Fritz, *Magic in the Ancient World.* (Cambridge, MA: Harvard University Press, 1999)

Grimal, Pierre, The Dictionary of Classical Mythology. (Trans A.R. Maxwell-Hyslop) (New York: Basil Blackwell Publisher, 1986)

Harrison, Jane Ellen, *Prolegomena: To the Study of Greek Religion* (Hardpress Publishing, 2013)

Hesiod, *Theogony/Works and Days*, Trans. M.L. West (Oxford: Oxford University Press, 1988)

Homer, *Iliad* Translated by A. T. Murray (1924 Loeb)

Homer, *Odyssey* Translated by A. T. Murray (1919 Loeb)

Homeric Hymns Translated by H. G. Evelyn-White (1914 Loeb)

Johnston, Sarah, *Restless Dead: Encounters Between the Living and the Dead in Ancient Greece*, (Berkeley: University of California Press, 1999)

Kerenyi, Karl, *The Gods of the Greeks,* (Thames and Hudson, 1980)

Kerenyi, Karl, *Eleusis: Archetypal Image of Mother and Daughter*, (Trans Ralph Manheim. Princeton, NJ: Princeton University Press, 1967)

Lewis, H. Jeremiah, *Gods and Mortals: New Stories of Hellenic Polytheism*

Martin, Thomas R. *Ancient Greece: From Prehistoric to Hellenistic Times* (Yale University Press; 2nd Ed, 2013)

Mikalson, Jon D., *Ancient Greek Religion.* (Imprint unknown; 2nd Revised Ed, 2011)

Murray, Gilbert, and Charles Twain, *Five Stages of Greek Religion: The History of Olympian Gods of Ancient Greece* (lulu.com, 2018)

Nilsson, Martin, *Greek Folk Religion,* (Gloucester: Peter Smith, 1971)

Nilsson, Martin, *History of Greek Religion,* (Trans F.J. Fielden.) (New York: W.W. Norton & Co., 1964)

Nilsson, Martin, *Greek Piety.* (Trans Herbert Rose) (New York: W.W. Norton & Co, 1969)

Ogden, Daniel, *Magic, Witchcraft and Ghosts in the Ancient Greek and Roman Worlds: A Sourcebook.* (Oxford University Press: 2nd Ed, 2009)

Panopoulous, Christo et al, *Hellenic Polytheism: Household Worship, Vol 1.* (CreateSpace Independent Publishing Platform; 1 ed, 2014)

Parke, H.W., *Festivals of the Athenians.* (London: Thames and Hudson, 1977)

Parker, Robert, C.T., *Miasma: Pollution and Purification in Early Greek Religion*

Pollard, John, *Seers, Shrines and Sirens: the Greek Religious Revolution in the Sixth Century B.C.* (London: George Allen & Unwin Ltd, 1965)

Prince, Simon, *Religions of the Ancient Greeks.* Cambridge: Cambridge University Press, 1997)

Pulleyn, Simon, *Prayer in Greek Religion.* (Oxford Classical Monographs) Clarenon Press, 1997

Rouse, William H.D., *Greek Votive Offerings.* (Cambridge: Cambridge University Press, 1902)

Simon, Erika, *Festivals of Attica.* (University of Wisconsin, 1983)

Stoneman, Richard, *The Ancient Oracles: Making the Gods Speak* (Yale University Press, 2011)

Winter, Sarah Kate Istra, *KHARIS: Hellenic Polytheism Explored* (USA: Cafepress.com 2004)

Winter, Sarah Kate Istra, *Komos: Celebrating Festivals in Contemporary Hellenic Polytheism* (CreateSpace Independent Publishing Platform, 2015)

Social Media/Websites/Blogs

You can find me on Instagram and Facebook – Starlit's Magical Corner is where I share my Hellenic journey and create Hellenic inspired magic and mysticism

Kitchen Witch School of Natural Witchery - kitchenwitchhearth. net/blog – I blog here sometimes on all kinds of things, sometimes Greek inspired! LOADS of amazing blogs on all things natural witchery

Theoi – theoi.com - An excellent online source for reference on the thousands of characters in Greek Myth

Elaion - baringtheaegis.blogspot.com - Go to this blog for all things concerning Hellenic Polytheism, including PAT Rituals

Hellenion – hellenion.org – nonprofit organisation, lots of resources and articles, memberships and a clergy training program

HMEPA – numachi.com/~ccount/hmepa – this little gem aligns the Attic Calendar with modern day calendars

Kharis – winterscapes.com/kharis/ - for one of my favourite authors Sarah Kate Istra Winter

Ancient Education - ancient.eu/ - if you're looking for brief overviews of all kinds of ancient history, excellent articles of Greek history

Labrys - labrys.gr/en/ - an emerging community of Hellenic Polytheists, practicing in Athens, in person events/rituals for anyone visiting Greece

Ancient Greek Religion – greekreligion.org – a huge collection of website links regards Hellenic Polytheism

Patheos Blog-https://www.patheos.com/blogs/hearthwitchdown under/author/bebel

**MOON
BOOKS**

PAGANISM & SHAMANISM

What is Paganism? A religion, a spirituality, an alternative belief system, nature worship? You can find support for all these definitions (and many more) in dictionaries, encyclopaedias, and text books of religion, but subscribe to any one and the truth will evade you. Above all Paganism is a creative pursuit, an encounter with reality, an exploration of meaning and an expression of the soul. Druids, Heathens, Wiccans and others, all contribute their insights and literary riches to the Pagan tradition. Moon Books invites you to begin or to deepen your own encounter, right here, right now.

If you have enjoyed this book, why not tell other readers by posting a review on your preferred book site.

Medicine for the Soul
The Complete Book of Shamanic Healing
Ross Heaven
All you will ever need to know about shamanic healing and how to
become your own shaman...
Paperback: 978-1-78099-419-2 ebook: 978-1-78099-420-8

Shaman Pathways – The Druid Shaman
Exploring the Celtic Otherworld
Danu Forest
A practical guide to Celtic shamanism with exercises and
techniques as well as traditional lore for exploring the Celtic
Otherworld.
Paperback: 978-1-78099-615-8 ebook: 978-1-78099-616-5

Traditional Witchcraft for the Woods and Forests
A Witch's Guide to the Woodland with Guided Meditations and
Pathworking
Mélusine Draco
A Witch's guide to walking alone in the woods, with guided
meditations and pathworking.
Paperback: 978-1-84694-803-9 ebook: 978-1-84694-804-6

Wild Earth, Wild Soul
A Manual for an Ecstatic Culture
Bill Pfeiffer
Imagine a nature-based culture so alive and so connected,
spreading like wildfire. This book is the first flame...
Paperback: 978-1-78099-187-0 ebook: 978-1-78099-188-7

Naming the Goddess
Trevor Greenfield
Naming the Goddess is written by over eighty adherents and
scholars of Goddess and Goddess Spirituality.
Paperback: 978-1-78279-476-9 ebook: 978-1-78279-475-2

Shapeshifting into Higher Consciousness
Heal and Transform Yourself and Our World with Ancient
Shamanic and Modern Methods
Llyn Roberts
Ancient and modern methods that you can use every day to
transform yourself and make a positive difference in the world.
Paperback: 978-1-84694-843-5 ebook: 978-1-84694-844-2

Readers of ebooks can buy or view any of these bestsellers by
clicking on the live link in the title. Most titles are published in
paperback and as an ebook. Paperbacks are available in traditional
bookshops. Both print and ebook formats are available online.

Find more titles and sign up to our readers' newsletter at
http://www.johnhuntpublishing.com/paganism
Follow us on Facebook at https://www.facebook.com/MoonBooks
and Twitter at https://twitter.com/MoonBooksJHP